ON THE TRAIL OF THE
WHALE

Foreword by
PAUL McCARTNEY

Written and Photographed by
MARK CARWARDINE

Also by Mark Carwardine:

Iceland: Nature's Meeting Place
Birds in Focus
The WWF Environment Handbook
The Nature of Zambia
The Nature of Zimbabwe
The Nature of Pakistan
The Encyclopedia of World Wildlife

With Douglas Adams:
Last Chance to See...

With John Craven:
Wildlife in the News

Children's books:
Whales, Dolphins and Porpoises
The Animal Atlas
Animal Opposites (series)
Where Animals Live
Looking at How Animals Live (series)
Explore the World of Amazing Animals
Finding Out about Animals (series)

In press:
Eyewitness Handbook: Whales, Dolphins and Porpoises

ON THE TRAIL OF THE
WHALE

MARK CARWARDINE

A Thunder Bay book
ON THE TRAIL OF THE WHALE

First published in Great Britain by Thunder Bay Publishing Co 1994

Text and photographs copyright © Mark Carwardine 1994

The moral right of the author has been asserted.

ISBN 1 899074 00 7

Designed by: Schermuly Design Co. London
Reproduction by Regent, Hong Kong
Printed and bound in England by Biddles

Thunder Bay Publishing Co
PO Box 235
Guildford
Surrey
GU2 5ZQ
England

For all the whale watchers in the Scoff-in-the-Loft:

Graham and Margaret, Andrew and Clare, Les and Lis,

Barry and Rosemary, Valerie and Jeff, and Jocie.

Thanks to Hughie the humpback for bringing us together.

With special thanks to Mark Edwards

Contents

Acknowledgements ——————————————— 8
Foreword ——————————————————— 10
Introduction ——————————————————— 12

1 OVER DEEPWATER CANYONS ———————— 18
Deep-diving sperm whales in New Zealand

2 THE TRINCOMALEE BLUES ———————— 36
Blue whales in war-torn Sri Lanka

3 BLAZING PADDLES ————————————— 48
Kayaking with grey whales in Mexico

4 KUJIRA! ———————————————————— 62
Bryde's whales and ex-whalers in Japan

5 THE SNORKEL PARTY ————————————— 76
Swimming with pilot whales in the Canary Islands

6 ORCA WATERS ———————————————— 88
Friendly killer whales in Canada

7 BIG-WINGED NEW ENGLANDER ————————— 98
Humpback whales off America's east coast

8 MINKE PATROL ———————————————— 118
Studying minke whales in Scotland

9 THE SWINGIN' HUMPBACKS ————————— 132
Singing humpback whales in Hawaii

10 BREACH FROM THE BED ————————— 142
Right whales from a hotel bed in South Africa

Appendices
Guidelines for whale watching ——————— 156
A note on photography ——————————— 157
Further information ———————————— 158

Acknowledgements

THIS BOOK would have been impossible to research and write without the generosity, advice and enthusiasm of a great many people. Some shared their knowledge; others read and commented on early versions of the text; and they all provided moral support and encouragement. I would like to thank everyone who has been involved.

I am particularly indebted to a number of people in England. Many thanks to Paul McCartney for writing such an appropriate and thought-provoking foreword. Doreen Montgomery gave me sound advice, although I did not realise it at the time. Pat Harrison's valuable contribution was much appreciated. Clive Stacey and Mark Leaney, my friends at Discover the World, were typically patient while I was incommunicado for weeks at a time. Sean Whyte, Eric Hoyt, Melanie Lamb, Vassili Papastavrou, Chris Stroud and Alison Smith helped in a great many ways and never once complained about my constant interruptions. Mark Edwards was originally going to do the photography but had to leave the task to me; no doubt he would have taken better pictures, but his advice and unerring enthusiasm were invaluable. Nick Middleton helped so much that he probably spent more time on my book than his own. Air New Zealand, South African Airways, SAS, American Airlines and Air Canada all helped with flights; Clare McKay and John Daniels were particularly supportive. Sue Colman, at Nikon UK, came to the rescue more than once. Hugh Schermuly was always efficient, helpful and full of good ideas – and willingly burnt the midnight oil. Debra Taylor was typically understanding and supportive. And last, but definitely not least, my parents very kindly provided a secret hideaway – safe from telephones, faxes, chocolate and other distractions from writing.

A huge number of people helped during my travels and many have become good friends. I hope I have not missed anyone from this list but, if I have, please accept my sincere apologies.

OVER DEEPWATER CANYONS: Richard Oliver, Craig Posa, Mike Howse, Morris Wanawatu, Marcus Solomon, Lorraine Hawke, Riria Kahu and Miriama Watson (all at Whale Watch Kaikoura Ltd); Rick Buurman, Dennis Buurman and Ian Bradshaw (Dolphin Mary Charters); Barbara Todd; Carol Seguin; Steve Hide (Kaikoura Star); Nigel Gee (Kaikoura Helitours); and Margo and 'Wix' Wickens.

THE TRINCOMALEE BLUES: Graham Thompson; Duncan Murrell; Dr. Hiran W. Jayewardene (Secretary-General, Indian Ocean Marine Affairs Co-operation); and Brian Lourensz (Chairman, Consolidated Marine Engineers Ltd).

BLAZING PADDLES: Steve Smith and Jim Allan (Ecosummer Expeditions).

KUJIRA!: Shigeki Komori and Mikako Awano (WWF-Japan); Nagaoka Tomohisa; and Moritoshi Hamasaki.

THE SNORKEL PARTY: Jim and Sara Heimlich-Boran.

ORCA WATERS: Bill MacKay and Jim Borrowman (Stubbs Island Charters).

BIG-WINGED NEW ENGLANDER: Mason Weinrich, Malcolm Martin and Rachel Classen (Cetacean Research Unit); Steve Sears, Jim Marr, Mark and Bill Cunningham and Colin Foster (Captain Bill's Whale Watch).

MINKE PATROL: Richard and Judy Fairbairns (Sea Life Cruises); Tom Walmsley; and Janine Booth.

THE SWINGIN' HUMPBACKS: Paul Forestell and Gregory Kaufman (Pacific Whale Foundation).

BREACH FROM THE BED: Nan Rice (Founder and Secretary, Dolphin Action & Protection Group); Dr. John Hanks, Brenda Crook and Jeanne Streicher (Southern African Nature Foundation); Brian Ancketill and Andree du Plessis (Hermanus Publicity Association); Pieter Claasen (The Old Harbour Museum); and Michael Olivier.

I have also been fortunate to share the company of several thousand fellow whale watchers around the world, sometimes for a few hours and occasionally for as long as several weeks. It has been a great pleasure to meet so many people with a similar love of whales.

Foreword

ON A RECENT CONCERT TOUR of the world I met a woman who said to me 'my ambition in life is to see a whale before I die'. I believe she is typical of a growing number of people who feel the same way - and who realise that it is becoming more and more possible to make this great ambition come true.

For many years now, my wife Linda and I (and our kids for that matter) have been strongly opposed to the killing of whales and, like many people, have been doing our utmost to save the largest creatures ever to grace our fair planet. In Norway, traditionally a whaling nation, we spoke out against what we see as the unnecessary slaughter of these precious animals. We were met with the objection that people had been making their living from whaling for countless generations. But our argument was that people once sold slaves for a living, and children were forced to work in mines. At the time, this was all thought to be perfectly acceptable. But we have moved on. We have learned that such behaviour is brutal and can lead only to a lack of regard for life in general.

Obviously, no-one wants to see people thrown out of work, particularly in these recessionary times, so an alternative way of making a living has to be found. Nowadays, there is a real alternative to whale slaughter – whale watching. I believe that well-organised whale watching will provide a perfectly acceptable method of making money for the whaling communities. It will also offer an opportunity for the people of the world to learn about these great creatures and to experience them living wild and free in their natural environment.

I hope Mark's book will inspire more people to achieve this great dream for themselves and that it will help to show us the way to a more peaceful and happier future.

Paul McCartney

Introduction

THIS IS THE STORY of a year spent travelling the world in search of whales. If there is anything to be learnt from the story, it is simply that there is no better way to spend a year, and nothing better to seek.

There is something about whales that grabs you by the scruff of the neck and makes you think about them morning, noon and night. At the risk of sounding theatrical, they transmit good vibes: they are surrounded by a strange mystical aura that, quite simply, makes you feel good.

I will never forget the spectacle of a 30-ton humpback whale launching itself high into the air, or the sight of a sperm whale diving into the murky depths thousands of feet below the boat. I can still hear the sound of a family of killer whales in animated conversation, and frequently dream about swimming with a group of inquisitive short-finned pilot whales. These are the kind of close encounters that stay with you for the rest of your life.

Just a brief flirtation with a whale is often all it takes to turn normal, quiet, unflappable people into delirious, jabbering extroverts. On whale watching trips, almost everyone becomes the life and soul of the party. I have seen grown men and women dance around the deck, break into song, burst into tears, slap one another on the back and do all the things that normal, quiet, unflappable people are not supposed to do. I have done them myself.

After a while, the jabbering and the delirium subside, but you are still left with a good feeling that never really wanes. Once you have seen a whale, there is an immense and lasting satisfaction in simply knowing that it is out there, wild and free.

The fact is that whale watching is addictive. It sneaks up on you and becomes an all-consuming, lifelong passion. I have been on many hundreds of whale watching trips, but every time I head out to sea I still get the same buzz of anticipation that I felt the first time around. When I see a whale I am floating, on a high, living on another planet. Even when I return to Earth, or at least to England, and am sitting watching the rain on a grey Monday morning, all I have to do is to cast my mind back... think of whales. I get the same uplifting feeling, the same good vibes, and I survive until Tuesday.

By now, if you have not already seen a whale, you may be wondering if I am short of a marble or two. I think if I had seen this introduction 17 years ago, before my first close encounter with a whale, I would have been wondering the same thing. But I hope that after reading this book you will think again. In the meantime, ask someone who *has* already seen a whale, because they will know exactly what I mean. You may not have realised it before now, but the world is brimming with 'whale junkies' - people who have to see a whale at frequent intervals just to survive their normal daily lives. So even if I am crazy, I am not alone.

At this point, I should explain the purpose of the book because, although no-one needs an excuse to go whale watching, I happened to have a good one. Here was the angle. I was to put a hand-picked menagerie of whale watching trips to the test, and then write about them. Not just about what happened, but about what it really felt like to meet the whales and to get to know them socially. During the course of these 'test drives', I also wanted to get into the whale watching psyche, to get to the bottom of this strange mystical aura that everyone (including me) kept talking about. I wanted to find out if whale watchers were the kind of people you could pick out in a police line-up, or if they were all manner of people from all walks of life.

I had more serious intentions as well: to do some detective work on behalf of the whales themselves. In particular, I wanted to delve deeper into their reactions to the whale watchers. I knew that my observations and conclusions would be subjective, but I wanted to consider whether they appeared to remain aloof and disinterested, if they found the crowds rather intimidating, or if they seemed to relish all the attention.

Choosing where to go was a challenge. I spent many a happy and frustrating hour fiddling around in my office in Guildford, sticking pins into a map of the world and trying to make up my mind. The problem was simple: so many places, so many whales, yet so little time. I wanted to watch as many different whales as possible in as many different ways as possible: from the air, from the shore and underwater, as well as from yachts, rubber inflatables, motor cruisers, fishing boats, research vessels, kayaks and even huge ocean-going ships. But it was more complicated than that, because I had to plan my itinerary around the whales themselves. The larger species tend to split their lives between widely separate feeding and breeding grounds, and rarely stay in one place for

A short-finned pilot whale in reflective mood.

more than a few months at a time. So I had to consult their diaries, before making any plans of my own, to ensure that I did not keep turning up at the right place at the wrong time. It would have been hopeless heading for Hawaii in the summer, for example, because all the humpbacks would have been in Alaska; and, likewise, if I had gone to South Africa in December, the southern right whales would have been a thousand miles away, eating their Christmas dinner in Antarctica. It was like trying to organise a day out with a group of travelling salesmen, only 365 times more complicated.

Choosing which whales to look for was another interesting dilemma. These days, there are so many commercial whale watching operations around the world that it is possible to see most of the larger species, and many of the smaller ones, simply by purchasing a ticket and keeping your fingers crossed. Blues, humpbacks, fins, minkes, southern rights, northern rights, greys and many others are all there for the watching.

Eventually, I stopped moving the pins around the map and plumped for ten different locations: Stellwagen Bank, an underwater plateau off the east coast of the United States; the war-torn town of Trincomalee, in north-eastern Sri Lanka; Baja California, along the wild Pacific coast of Mexico; Shikoku Island, in Japan; the picturesque island of Maui, in Hawaii; the package holiday paradise of Tenerife, in the Canary Islands; Canada's beautiful Vancouver Island; a sleepy little town called Kaikoura, in New Zealand; the wet and windy Isle of Mull, off the rugged west coast of Scotland; and a town called Hermanus, the 'whale capital' of South Africa.

I tried to squeeze in visits to Peninsula Valdes (Patagonia), Glacier Bay (Alaska), the St. Lawrence River (Canada), Hervey Bay (Australia) and several other whale watching meccas around the world. But time and money constraints got the better of me and, at the end of the day, I decided to postpone them for another time, another book. My final selection did manage to produce the goods: ten different species of whale, eight different dolphins and two species of porpoise... not bad for a few pins on a map.

I never travelled alone. Four million people came with me. Actually, to be honest, that is not strictly true. What really happened was that four million people went on commercial whale watching trips during the same year as me. But I did meet several thousand of them – from first-timers, on half-day tours where the whales were virtually guaranteed, to the kind of serious whale junkies who fly thousands of miles, part with large sums of money, brave seasickness and stormy weather and, of course, risk the disappointment of failing to see the featured attraction.

On average, every day of the year, nearly 15,000 people are out on the water watching whales. Yet it is quite a new phenomenon. Commercial whale watching began as recently as the mid-1950s, when people first started taking an interest in grey whales migrating along the coast of southern California. Even so, it was still many years before the gentle giants really grabbed everyone's attention. When I saw my first grey, in the rolling Pacific surf near Santa Monica, in 1978, whale watching was still small-fry compared to all the other attractions that southern California had to offer; and, outside North America, trips to see whales were few and far between. But nowadays whale watching seems to be the flavour of the decade, a rival for bird watching and the basis of a burgeoning multi-million pound industry involving nearly 40 different countries. The 1990s will always be remembered as the *whale rush years*: worldwide ticket sales exceeded £50 million in 1992 alone and, when accommodation, food and other essential bits and pieces are included as well, whale watching generated a total income of over £200 million.

The risk, of course, is that all these human admirers will love the whales to death. It is sometimes easy to forget that we are uninvited guests in their world and we are privileged to see them. We do not have a divine right. In fact, we have a responsibility to cause as little disturbance as possible: whale watching should be an eyes-on-hands-off activity and proper respect and etiquette are the most important tools of the trade.

We also have a responsibility to help the whales benefit from the whale rush as much as their guests. They will never be able to get their flippers on the money: it is not as if we can pay them a salary. We could not even guarantee to protect them from harpoons and drift nets, or promise never again to pollute their homes or pinch their fish. But what we can do is to ensure that part of the income from whale watching helps to fund the marine research and conservation projects that tackle these issues. We can even use the whale watching boats as platforms for research: there have been many studies on dead whales, but surprisingly little is known about live ones; modern technology has taken us to the Moon and beyond, but we are only just beginning to understand these extraordinary forms of intelligent life on our own planet.

We can also drum up public support for their cause. The whales themselves make terrific ambassadors for marine conservation. They light an internal fire that makes people determined to do something positive to help and they make a strong political argument for

A humpback whale drumming up support for its cause.

establishing marine nature reserves and other protected areas. It is up to the on-board naturalists, who should accompany every whale watching trip, to ensure that their captive audiences are kept well-informed.

There is another, more direct, benefit which is perhaps the most dramatic and exciting of them all. Whale watching, quite simply, is a valid counter-argument to whaling. All of a sudden, it is possible to make money from whales without having to kill them.

It is difficult to compare the profit-making potential of these two industries (what would be the price tag on four million happy and well-informed people?) but, if they were both awarded points, whale watching would walk off with the prize every time. First of all, it scores for turning normal, quiet, unflappable people into whale junkies and, if they were not already, into dedicated conservationists. It wins some more points for sharing out the profits with hoteliers, restaurateurs, shopkeepers and many other people, instead of among a select few people directly involved in whaling. But the really big points go for side-stepping the need to kill. This is a godsend for the whales, of course, but it is also good news for the local people – whales that are watched, not hunted, provide a source of income for life.

In some parts of the world, it is the old whaling vessels themselves that now leave the harbours armed, not with whalers and harpoons, but with tourists and cameras. We hunted whales without pity, and with cruel, explosive harpoons, until they were on the verge of extinction. We are still hunting them today, albeit on a smaller scale. Yet many whales show a striking – and deeply moving – level of trust. Some of the older bulls, are still wary and elusive (such an attitude once had survival value) but it is strange and wonderful to know that many of the others so readily accept us as friends.

If you are already a whale junkie, and you have seen humpbacks, greys, fins or any of the other great whales, I hope the stories that follow will bring back many happy memories.

If you have never had a close encounter with a whale, I hope they will inspire you to get out and meet one. You will not be disappointed.

Over Deepwater Canyons

DEEP-DIVING SPERM WHALES IN NEW ZEALAND

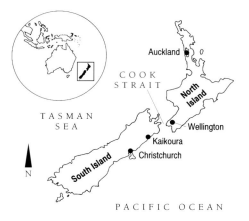

AFTER A BOMB SCARE at the airport, crossing the international date line (I never did work out what happened to Tuesday 10th November), a 24-hour flight to Auckland, an internal flight to Wellington, a three-hour ferry journey across Cook Strait and a 100-mile drive in a hire car, I arrived in Kaikoura a little the worse for wear.

But the stresses and strains of travel melted away the moment I rolled into town. Kaikoura is the kind of place where people sit on their front porches every evening to watch the light fade over the South Pacific. Time passes slowly and peacefully while they wait for something to happen. Nothing ever does happen, of course, but after a while it no longer seems to matter: in Kaikoura, people live life at the pace it was meant to be lived.

Lying roughly midway between Wellington and Christchurch, on the east coast of South Island, New Zealand, it is a pleasant little town sandwiched between the sea and a spectacular range of snow-capped mountains. It is the meeting point of two opposing currents which fuel a highly productive food chain just offshore. A warm current from the north meets a cold one from the south and, together, they lift nutrients

18

from the seabed up towards the surface. These provide sustenance for microscopic plants, which are eaten by small animals which, in turn, are eaten by fish, seabirds, seals and whales.

It was the abundance of whales that first attracted European settlers to Kaikoura. The town grew from a shore-based whaling station, established in 1843, and the whaling continued on and off until the early 1960s. The last whale killed by a New Zealand vessel was a bull sperm whale off the Kaikoura coast in 1964.

Nowadays, the animals are fully protected and whale watching, not hunting, is the focus of attention. Since commercial operations began in 1988, Kaikoura has become a magnet for whale watchers from all over the world. The animals attract some 30,000 people to the town every year, and have already paved the way for nearly 50 new businesses (including hotels, restaurants and shops) and, consequently, they have helped to create scores of new jobs. The visitors come to see a resident group of sperm whales, which live literally within sight of the town. It is one of the few places where these extraordinary animals, perhaps the strangest of all the great whales, are so readily accessible from shore.

It was my first full day in Kaikoura and I was in a 20-foot rigid-hulled inflatable boat, slowly being smashed to a pulp. Standing at the front, next to skipper Richard Oliver, I was on a shock-absorbing foam mat. But the mat was useless. Every time we hurtled over the crest of a wave, and free-fell down the other side, it felt as if we had been standing in an elevator when the cable had snapped. The only difference was that, instead of being carried away on a stretcher and given a few days off work, we were thrown back in and winched up ready for the cable to snap again. And again, and again. We had been on the water for less than ten minutes but already I was battered and bruised. The best I could do was to hold on tight enough to prevent my legs or, worse still, my back from suddenly bending in a way they were not designed to bend.

Richard was used to it: he was about to embark on his 2,000th whale watch. He did these three-hour trips as many as four times a day, seven days a week, and had experienced more than his fair share of pummelling. On a similar ride earlier in the year, he was bounced around so badly that he lost his stomach. He did not actually lose it, of course. I am exaggerating. But it slipped out of place and had to be coaxed back into its original position by a doctor.

Meanwhile, by comparison, all the other passengers were travelling first-class. There were 12 of them, strapped safely into bright orange lifejackets, and sitting in comfortable seats behind us. They were too far back to feel the worst of the ride and, according to one man, the sensation was rather like being in a washing machine on the spin cycle. They whooped and cheered when we crashed over the waves and grimaced every time I cracked my head against the metal roof of the cabin.

A frothy wake chased us out towards the whale watching grounds, south of Kaikoura, at a speed of about 35 miles per hour. We were heading for a series of deep underwater canyons which run through the area (in places less than half a mile from town) and drop to depths of between 3,000 and 5,000 feet. The canyons themselves are remote and mysterious – we probably know more about the dark side of the Moon – but they are ideal sperm whale country.

Sperm whales hunt in these extreme depths for large deepwater fish and squid. They are the only great whales with teeth and make up for all their toothless relatives by having particularly large ones; each can weigh over two pounds. (Even sperm whales do not have teeth in their upper jaws, though, preferring to pack up to 50 in two parallel rows along their narrow, underslung lower jaws).

Still within sight of town, Richard stopped the boat. We quickly grabbed our cameras and stood up, expecting to see a whale, but the only signs of life were a lone cape petrel gliding past and a wandering albatross wheeling and turning in the distance. Richard smiled apologetically and explained that sperm whales are notoriously difficult animals to find. Watching them, he told us, requires patience, experience and a fair amount of luck.

The problem is that they behave like submarines, and spend most of their lives underwater. Some sperm whales can hold their breath for more than two hours at a time and they have been recorded at depths of nearly two miles. The average dive time off the coast of Kaikoura is 40-45 minutes, but then they rarely spend more than 10 or 12 minutes on the surface before diving again. So, unless you happen to be in the right place at the right time – which is next to the whale when it comes up to the surface briefly to breathe – the chances of a close encounter are fairly remote.

We stared at the vast expanse of empty water in despair. The thought of rolling around in the swell for several hours, hoping for a sperm whale to appear within sight or sound of the boat, did not appeal.

But Richard is not a man to sit around and wait. He told us about an ingenious piece of whale-finding equipment which enables him to find the animals on almost every trip. By listening to their activities underwater he can judge where they are most likely to surface and therefore, against all the odds, he can almost *guarantee* to be in the right place at the right time.

We were most impressed. At least we were, until he pulled out the strange contraption from underneath his seat. A scientist would have called it a 'directional hydrophone', which is a kind of underwater microphone used to tell where sounds are coming from. But that seemed too grand a term for what basically consisted of a ski pole, part of an old telephone, some fibreglass resin and a pair of second-hand headphones.

Several people were looking at Richard as though he was completely mad. Undeterred, he put the headphones over his ears, held the ski pole by its rubber handle and leaned over the side of the boat. At the end of the pole was a small microphone (taken from the telephone handset) and this had been encased in the fibreglass resin to make it waterproof. As we watched with growing suspicion, he stuck the pole in the water, paused to listen for a moment, turned it around 90 degrees and listened again. Frowning with concentration, he turned it another 90 degrees and listened yet again. Then he stood up and, with a knowing smile, announced that there were two whales in the area, one a little way offshore and the other a bit further south. Resting the ski pole on the side of the boat, he turned on the ignition, headed south for about a quarter of a mile and stopped again. This time he handed the headphones to me. Despite my reservations about his whale-finding equipment, I desperately wanted to hear something and just managed to make out a muffled clicking sound that seemed to be coming from somewhere between the boat and the shore, although it was very hard to tell. It was a monotonous sound, repeated about once every second or two, rather like a metronome tapping out a slow, melancholic beat. I rotated the hydrophone, listening for the clicks to get stronger, until I thought it was pointing straight at the whale. Richard listened briefly to check that I was right (I was, well, nearly) and turned the boat towards the sound. He stopped for a third time, had one more listen and, finally, seemed to be satisfied. We had about a five minute wait, he reckoned, though I do not think anyone on board was really sure whether to believe him or not.

As we bobbed around on the surface, a Japanese couple were being sick overboard (for some inexplicable reason, the Japanese seem to suffer from seasickness more than most other nationalities) and the rest of us tried to take our minds off their predicament by trying to imagine what the whale might be doing instead. With the help of Richard's hydrophone we eavesdropped on its activities in the cold, dark canyon hundreds, or perhaps thousands, of feet below us.

No-one has ever seen a sperm whale at such depths, of course, because even in a submarine there would be little chance of finding one in the inky blackness. But the clicking can give away some interesting clues about its activities. Varied clicks, like Morse code, would suggest that it was talking to another whale, perhaps too far away for us to hear the reply. A loud 'clang', like an echoing gunshot, would probably mean that it was checking for boats and other obstructions on the surface. A series of extra-loud clicks may be used to stun its prey, as if it were firing invisible bullets. And rapid-fire clicks, like the creaking of an old wooden door, followed by silence, are believed to be made when it is homing in on a fish or squid and then eating its catch; this is probably the most awe-inspiring sound of them all – something which whale expert Barbara Todd, who has been studying Kaikoura's sperm whales for many years, calls the 'click, click, click, gulp' theory.

The whale below us was sending out a steady pulse of sound. It was 'scanning' or 'searching', like a bat finding its way around in the dark. After a few minutes, the scanning became noticeably slower, with about four or five seconds between each click, and then it stopped altogether. The whale was about to surface.

Richard spotted it first and, as he pointed, the rest of us caught a glimpse of the second blow. Each species of whale has its own distinctive blow: the sperm's is low and bushy and angled slightly forward; it also projects to the left, because the blowhole is on the left side of the head. But from a distance of several hundred yards, it was impossible to see much more than what appeared to be a quick puff of smoke - and it seemed to be coming straight out of the sea. Hidden in the swell, the whale itself was invisible.

Whale watching in New Zealand is strictly controlled by the Marine Mammal Protection Regulations, which draw two imaginary lines around every animal. The first is about 300 yards away and marks the point where boats have to slow down to a 'no wake' speed. The second is about 50 yards away and marks the boundary of a 'no-go' area. The aim is to give the whales some personal space while still allowing their admirers a good view. If the whales choose to come any closer, that is entirely up to them and the boats simply have to stay still. On the other hand, anyone seen actively approaching a whale too closely, and therefore breaking the law, can be fined up to NZ$10,000 and is likely to have the boat confiscated. But the staff of Whale Watch Kaikoura Ltd are more interested in the welfare of the animals than the risk of fines or confiscations. The skippers and guides often spend more time with the whales than they do with their own families – and seem to look after them with about as much dedication.

We meandered towards 'our' whale from the side (sperm whales do not like being approached from immediately behind) and Richard recognised him as an old friend called Knuckles. Named after two distinctive bumps in front of his dorsal fin, he was lying perfectly still in the water and either failed to register our approach or simply pretended not to notice. He continued breathing steadily, about three or four times every minute, forcing a tremendous whoosh of air and water droplets out of his blowhole with each exhalation.

Knuckles was a bachelor. Probably born somewhere in the tropical South Pacific, he was at that difficult age - too old to be living with his mother but not old enough to find a willing female and start a family of his own. Basically, he was a teenager with a 10 or 15 year sabbatical before his life really started to get interesting. One day, he will leave the Kaikoura area to spend his first winter at the sperm whale breeding grounds in warmer seas further north. But in the meantime, his days (and possibly his nights – no-one really knows) consist of a dive and a good hearty meal, followed by a rest; then another dive and a good hearty meal, followed by another rest; and then another dive and a good hearty meal, and a rest, and so on in a relentless cycle until he is big and strong enough to win himself a wife (or, if he can manage it, several wives). Like many of the whales around Kaikoura, he is there for no better reason than to get bigger, older and wiser.

He looked quite big already. On the surface, sperm whales display less than two thirds of their overall length: all that was visible of Knuckles was the top of his head and a small portion of his back. But what little we could see was considerably longer than our boat. We tried to estimate his length with the help of an old rule of thumb used by whalers many years ago. They said that for every foot of a sperm whale's length it will breath once at the surface and spend about a minute underwater during its next dive. So a 50-foot whale would take about 50 breaths at the surface and then dive for 50 minutes. We counted a total of 38 breaths and therefore estimated a length of 38 feet. That would have made him almost twice the length of the boat, which seemed about right. By the time he is fully grown he could be more than 60 feet and weigh as much as 50 tons.

We wondered how long he had just spent hunting in the cold depths (perhaps it really was 38 minutes?) and watched in silent admiration as he replenished his oxygen supply for another dive. He barely moved. In fact, were it not for his periodic blows, I would scarcely have known he was alive.

It was little more than ten minutes before Knuckles started to prepare for his next foray into the canyon. He stretched a few times, like a marathon runner getting ready for a big race, then arched his back slightly and dropped out of sight. At first, we thought he had dived already. But he was accelerating forward, just a couple of feet below the surface, and soon reappeared a few yards further on. This time he arched his back more strongly and, in one graceful movement, lifted his enormous tail high into the air. Several people gasped, some cameras clicked and Knuckles, barely creating a ripple, disappeared into the murky depths.

In between whale watching, I sat at the Whaleway Station Café, drinking coffee, eating cakes, talking about whales and watching one of the smallest and rarest members of the dolphin family.

The cafe inhabits the back of a beach on the northern side of town and is probably the best place in the world to see Hector's dolphins. It is certainly the most unlikely place to see them: most other dolphins expect you to invest at least a modicum of effort, and an exhilarating ride in a boat, before they are prepared to show themselves. But by sitting outside on the verandah, and carefully scanning the shoreline, it was usually possible to see three or four Hector's dolphins in the time it took to drink a single cup of coffee. There are not many cafes where this would be possible, if only because Hector's dolphins are extremely rare (there may be fewer than 3,000 left) and because they are found only in New Zealand. On a calm day, if the Whaleway Station was almost empty, or if all the customers were unusually quiet, I could hear the dolphins' puffing breaths even before their unmistakably dark, rounded dorsal fins came into view. Whenever there were two of them swimming side-by-side, their fins resembled Mickey Mouse's ears; and, strangely, as they bobbed up and down on the surface of the water, it looked as if Mickey was drowning.

Almost within sight and sound of the Whaleway Station Cafe was another kind of dolphin – a wild bottlenose dolphin called Maui. She had arrived in town two months earlier, in August 1992, and by the time I returned to Kaikoura the following March had become a popular member of the local community. I expect by now she has been awarded honorary citizenship.

Bottlenose dolphins are occasionally seen many miles offshore but seldom around Kaikoura itself, so no-one knows where she came from. She may have been separated from her school during a storm, or perhaps she was just a lone wanderer and, like many casual visitors to Kaikoura, simply fell in love with the place and decided to stay.

The first time we met, she was spending most of her time in a secluded bay on the outskirts of town, and I used to watch her from the Old Wharf. There was usually a crowd of people there: Maui was rarely

Maui playing in her jacuzzi

without an audience. Every time a boat came around the Kaikoura Peninsula, she would rush out to say 'hello', leaping and splashing alongside before guiding it safely back into the bay.

When I saw her the second time, she had grown considerably broader and nearly a foot longer, making her roughly nine feet in length and surprisingly stocky. She was also much bolder and had developed a dangerous fascination for boats' propellers. She loved swimming in the wash behind some of the faster boats with her nose inches away from the spinning blades, or lying upside-down in the foam as if she were having a jacuzzi. It was a risky business; her nose and back were covered with tiny nicks and scars and there was a sizeable chunk missing from her chin. She had one particularly nasty scar on her side, the result of such a terrible propeller injury that, at the time, everyone thought she was going to die.

Unfortunately, she does not seem to have learnt the lesson. As we came around the Peninsula, in one of the Whale Watch inflatables, she appeared on cue (you never have to find Maui: she always finds you) and, within seconds, was experimenting to see how close she could swim to the propeller without chopping the end of her snout into lots of little pieces. It was scary to watch. We continued around to the Old Wharf and slowed down, being careful not to make any sudden movements. Maui, very wisely, slowed down too. She seemed pleased to see us and, as soon as we had stopped, leaped out of the water next to the boat. I swear she was looking to see if she recognised anyone on board. There were six of us altogether: Craig Posa and Carol Seguin, two of her closest friends; Sean Whyte, Director of the UK-based Whale and Dolphin Conservation Society; Paul and Margo Wickens (Paul is the keyboard player in Paul McCartney's band and was taking a couple of days off in the middle of a hectic world tour); and myself.

Craig and Carol swim with Maui almost every evening (imagine... some people watch television, others swim with a wild bottlenose dolphin) and she trusts them both implicitly. She is so fond of Carol, in particular, that she tends to ignore everyone else in the water: she offers her human friend gifts of seaweed, lies on one side waiting to be tickled and even gives her free underwater rides. There can be half a dozen people desperately keen to swim with her, but Carol receives all the attention.

So while Paul and I went in for a swim, poor Carol magnanimously volunteered to stay on the boat, well out of sight.

At first, Maui circled and prodded us a few times, like an airport official looking over a pair of scruffy, suspicious-looking passengers and checking their passports. Apparently satisfied, she dived into the darkness below and disappeared from view. A moment later she reappeared, kicking her tail hard and heading straight for the surface. She missed us by no more than a couple of feet and leaped out of the water right over our heads. Then she started showing off: swimming upside-down, spinning around in circles, kicking hard and raising half her body out of the water, slapping the surface with her tail and leaping high into the air. Sometimes we were allowed to join in her fun and games, though often they were too fast and confusing so we just watched, spellbound, from the sidelines.

Every once in a while she stopped what she was doing and swam over to examine the boat's propeller. She simply could not work out why it was staying so still and desperately wanted to get it moving again. She rubbed it with her chin, then she pulled back a little and prodded it with her snout. It was still refusing to budge, so she swam around in a slow, full circle and, with the concentration of a surgeon, gave it a close and careful examination. She even turned upside-down to look at it from an entirely different angle. She prodded and pushed again and seemed to be getting increasingly frustrated. After each failure, she dived out of sight below the boat (perhaps to let off steam) and reappeared a few moments later. Her best effort was when she took a deep breath, positioned herself immediately underneath the propeller and blew a stream of bubbles to try and force the blades to turn around. It was a clever idea, but still nothing happened and, eventually, she gave up.

Turning her attentions back to her two-man audience, still underwater and avidly watching her every move, she swam straight towards me and peered inquisitively into my mask from just a few inches away. Then she nibbled at the mouthpiece of my snorkel. She suddenly noticed Paul, who was holding a piece of seaweed, and swam over to join him. Paul's head was out of the water and Maui poked her head out too, allowing him to drape the seaweed over her long snout. She paused for a moment, tossed it into the air and then waited patiently for him to pick it up and start the game all over again. It was like playing 'fetch' with a dog, except the dog was throwing the stick.

She allowed us to tickle her under the chin, stroke her back (her skin was silky smooth to touch) and rub her snout. If at any moment we dared to stop she jerked her head in complaint and waited for us to carry on a bit longer.

The water was freezing cold, but we hardly noticed the minutes, and then more than an hour, tick rapidly by. We dragged ourselves away only when the sun dropped below the horizon and it was getting too dark to see what was happening. Numb and almost speechless as the others hauled us back on board, Paul summed up the swim perfectly. His lifelong ambition had always been to play at Madison Square Garden, in New York, and a couple of years ago his dream came true. With Paul McCartney and the band he played in front of a phenomenal 20,000 people. It was an experience he will never forget. But that buzz, the euphoria, the ecstasy - it was all overshadowed by swimming with Maui. Whales and dolphins have a habit of affecting people like that.

The next time I saw a sperm whale was from a height of about 1,000 feet. I was leaning out of a helicopter trying to photograph a new arrival called No-name. This was only a temporary name, of course, but it was something to be getting on with for the time being, at least until he revealed a sufficiently distinctive trait to be given a more descriptive one.

(During my second visit to Kaikoura several months later I discovered that he had been christened 'Mark'. I was inordinately proud, though just a little perturbed, when everyone jokingly declined to reveal which traits, in particular, No-name and I had in common).

Nigel Gee, the helicopter pilot, had removed the passenger door to give me a better view and, strapped in tightly, I could lean out to see the whale directly below me. For the first time, from this unique perspective, I really grasped a sperm whale's true size and shape. It was No-name's enormous blunt head that really caught my eye. It must have been about 15 feet long, or a third the length of his body.

The head contains a huge cavity with a tangle of hollow, web-like pipes inside. These are filled with a viscous liquid called spermaceti oil. Early whalers mistook this valuable oil for sperm – naming the whale accordingly – and sold it to be used as a lubricant, in leather tanning, as a lamp fuel and in the chemical industry. The whales themselves probably use it for buoyancy control. According to one theory, water is sucked in through the blowhole to cool the liquid and turn it into a wax; since this is denser than oil it helps the animal to sink. At the end of a dive, the water is flushed out and replaced with warm blood, which warms the wax and turns it back into an oil; this makes the whale more buoyant and helps it to rise back up to the surface. It is an ingenious system that possibly saves a great deal of energy when the whale is moving up or down in the water.

The star of Herman Melville's classic 19th century novel *Moby Dick*, the sperm whale is the species that most people probably associate with the word 'whale'. Melville was once a whaler himself and his story describes a mythical great white sperm whale being pursued across the high seas by a whaling ship. No-name was a real-life Moby Dick, but albino whales are rare and he was actually dark grey in colour. Like all sperm whales, he had a strangely wrinkled skin. It was especially noticeable from above and I remember thinking that it made him look like a long, dried prune. From my high vantage point, even his tail was clearly visible just below the surface; it looked powerful and broad, with a wavy trailing edge and a distinctive 'V' cut in the middle.

No-name had been surprisingly difficult to see from a distance. Nigel was an expert and found him incredibly quickly, but to me his blows looked deceptively like enormous whitecaps and, until we were almost overhead, I could barely tell his wrinkled body from ripples on the water. As we approached, he did not seem to respond to the helicopter at all. He continued breathing at a steady rate – I could see his single, dark, slit-like blowhole opening and closing with every breath – and he remained quite motionless, calmly preparing for his next dive. It was a full ten minutes before he lifted his tail high into the air, and disappeared from sight.

Like the boats, with their two imaginary lines drawn around every whale, helicopters and light aircraft are also governed by strict regulations. They are banned from descending too low over the animals, with a legal limit of 1,000 feet. The New Zealand Department of Conservation ensures that everyone – pilots and skippers alike – adheres to the letter of the law. With the help of frequent spot-checks by plain clothes conservation officers, it makes sure that whale watching in Kaikoura is conducted to a very high standard.

One helicopter, two light aircraft and four boats are currently licensed to take people whale watching in the area. But the licensing has been the subject of heated debate for some time. Whale Watch Kaikoura is a community trust owned jointly by the Maori people of the town and their affiliated tribe, the Ngai Tahu. They dispute the Department of

Conservation's right to issue permits which, obviously, are worth a great deal of money. Citing ancient aboriginal entitlements and, in particular, an agreement called the Treaty of Waitangi as evidence, they claim an exclusive right to issue new permits themselves. (Signed in 1840, the Treaty of Waitangi is widely accepted as New Zealand's founding document; basically, it is an agreement with the British Crown that grants the rights of the Queen to 'govern' New Zealand and guarantees the Maori people possession of their land, forests, fisheries and other natural resources).

It is a difficult and contentious issue that has yet to be resolved. But, in many ways, the real question should not be who has the right to issue new permits but whether or not more should be issued at all. The problem is that, although several studies have investigated the effect of whale watching on the whales (the latest involved 40 days at sea and no fewer than 272 close encounters) there is so much variation in the behaviour of individual whales that it has been impossible for the studies to draw many firm conclusions.

One of the most important considerations in Kaikoura is that the whale watching concentrates on just a handful of whales. During a single year, as many as 80 sperm whales move in and out of the area - but fewer than 20 of these are encountered on a regular basis. Some people argue that this is a perfect situation, because the 'regulars' become more tolerant of whale watching while the others are largely unaffected. But others argue that the better-known whales are rarely left alone because, during daylight hours, almost every time they come up to breathe there is likely to be a boat nearby or an aircraft overhead. It is possible, of course, that if the whales felt they were being harassed they could leave Kaikoura and join their colleagues further offshore; but no-one knows if there are territories involved, or if they would be accepted.

During a typical whale watching trip, most of the animals spotted are on their own. It is possible to watch one whale on the surface and, as soon as it has dived, move to a second and, with a little luck, onto a third - all in the space of a couple of hours. On the other hand, there may be several whales 'working' a small area together, in which case they tend to coordinate their dive times, surfacing and diving within minutes of each other; it is incredibly frustrating to pick up three or four animals on the hydrophone, only to be able to watch just one before they all go down for another three-quarters of an hour.

On a couple of occasions, I was lucky enough to see three different whales on a single trip. The first time there was Groove, White Dot and Hoon, then later I saw Hook, Scarface and No. 11 (named after two white marks on his dorsal fin).

We found Scarface within eight minutes of leaving the slipway, which must have been close to a record. It was sheer luck, because he just happened to surface right next to the boat before we had even started listening for clicks. We were in the *Uruao*, which is the largest of the whale watching vessels in Kaikoura, and the one which Scarface seemed to prefer. Named after a legendary guiding star for early Polynesian explorers, the *Uruao* is just over 40 feet long and, although a rigid-hulled inflatable like its smaller cousins, gives a much smoother ride. Helmed from a flying bridge and driven by three 250 horsepower outboard engines, it has a capacity for 30 passengers.

When Scarface dived, he dropped like a lead weight towards the seabed.

Every whale watching trip is accompanied by a naturalist-guide and, on this occasion, Lorraine Hawke was doing the commentary. She was sitting on the side of the boat, with her back to Scarface, explaining why there were sperm whales in the area and what this one, in particular, was doing on the surface. For a moment, she was so engrossed in her narrative that she did not notice Scarface making his way over to the boat to have a listen himself. He approached to within 30 feet and suddenly blew an explosive breath of smelly saltwater spray that soaked Lorraine from head to toe.

Scarface was named after a deep scar running all the way along the top of his head and we could see it clearly as he lolled in the water alongside the boat. Male sperm whales often have a large number of scars on their heads, caused by fights with other whales or by the hooks and suckers of giant squid. A fully-grown sperm whale needs to eat more than a ton of squid every day so, in theory, catching one big one makes more sense than trying to capture thousands of smaller ones. But giant squid are not just big - they are positively colossal. They can grow to more than 60 feet in length and, since they do not like being eaten, make intimidating adversaries. In a true battle of the giants, a stroppy squid will sometimes turn on a sperm whale and fiercely resist capture. In some cases, both animals die.

The water was fairly clear and, as Scarface dived, we could see him dip his head and drop straight down like a lead weight. In less than a minute, he would have been at 300 feet and still falling. In about ten minutes he would arrive in the cold, dark depths of a submarine canyon thousands of feet below. (As a sperm whale dives, its lungs collapse and the remaining air is forced out of them into the windpipe and nasal passages. It is able to keep swimming because of a vast store of oxygen in its muscles and in the blood; but even this is used wisely, as its heartbeat slows down and the oxygen is sent only to the brain and parts of the body that need it the most).

My favourite sperm whale was a rather freaky one called Schizo. Actually, his real name was Spotty, because he was covered in white spots, but his nickname was Schizo. I think Schizo was more appropriate, although it did seem a little unkind.

I met him only once. As we drifted alongside, he seemed like a perfectly normal sperm whale. He was lying in the water next to the boat, catching his breath after a long dive and quietly minding his own business. But that was the trouble with Schizo. He was unpredictable. One moment he was fine, the next he was as mad as a March hare. Perhaps he was the victim of too many whale watchers? Or, more likely, he had probably always been a little deranged.

Apparently, on one particular occasion, he head-butted a boat and then followed it around for more than 20 minutes. Every time the boat stopped, Schizo stopped too. Every time the boat went round in circles, Schizo went round in circles too. When the skipper began to get a little worried, and attempted to hide behind another boat, Schizo dived underneath and hid there too.

One of his favourite tricks, whenever a whale watching boat came alongside, was to turn and face the other way. It did not seem to matter which way he was facing in the first place, he always turned – as if it were a matter of principle rather than a good tactical move. Another trick was to lie upside-down about a foot underneath the hull of a boat, and then wait. No-one knew what he was waiting for but, in the interests of his own safety, the boat always had to stay perfectly still until he had finished.

With Schizo's undisputed reputation, we desperately wanted him to do something whacky. But we waited for ten minutes and nothing happened. We waited for another ten minutes and still nothing happened. Most normal whales would have dived long ago, but we decided to wait just a little longer. Still nothing happened. Eventually, after an hour and a half, we gave up and returned to shore, leaving Schizo all alone in a quiet world of his own.

What makes people get up at 5.30 in the morning, squeeze themselves into a cold, damp wetsuit, take a bumpy boat ride several miles out to sea and then jump into the freezing swell, in water 3,000 feet deep? Suicide is a possibility, though I doubt if that would require a wetsuit. I did it for a different reason - for a chance to swim with dusky dolphins.

It was barely light when I joined a small group of like-minded people, all still half asleep, in a boat called the *Dolphin Encounter*. But it was easily worth the early start. Within half an hour of leaving the jetty, we were idling into the outside edge of a school of several hundred boisterous duskies.

They were doing high double somersaults, low leaps, arc-shaped dives, surface lunges, belly-flops and a variety of other spirited acrobatics all around the boat. Every time one dolphin tried a new manoeuvre it seemed to catch on and, within minutes, all the others were practising the same trick. Sometimes they even synchronised their twisting and jumping, with perfect split-second timing that would have been the envy of a professional acrobat.

OVER DEEPWATER CANYONS –
New Zealand

LEFT: *Dusky dolphins are gregarious creatures by nature and often seek out the company of other dolphins and whales, seals... and people.*

RIGHT: *Listening for sperm whales with a ski pole, part of an old telephone, some fibreglass resin and a pair of headphones.*

BELOW: *Sperm whales have seriously wrinkled skin, making them resemble long dried prunes.*

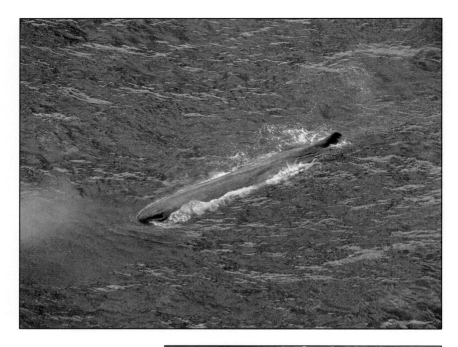

ABOVE: *Helicopter's eye view of the newly-named Mark; no-one would reveal which trait, in particular, we had in common.*

RIGHT: *You never have to find Maui: she always finds you.*

ABOVE: *Sperm whales behave like submarines and spend most of their lives underwater; this one is diving.*

BELOW: *On Rick's advice, I sang songs through my snorkel and, sure enough, the dusky dolphins came to have a closer look; I swear I even heard one of them whistle and click.*

RIGHT: *A dusky dolphin showing off its go-faster stripes.*

BELOW: *Sperm whale and sperm whale watchers happening to be in the same place at the same time.*

BELOW: *The ultimate in camouflage: a sperm whale mimics part of the Kaikoura mountain range.*

RIGHT: *Hungry fur seal, unfortunate octopus, and the reason why.*

BELOW: *Sitting at the Whaleway Station Café, it was usually possible to see three or four Hector's dolphins in the time it took to drink a single cup of coffee.*

ABOVE: *A sperm whale admires the spectacular view that makes whale watching in Kaikoura so unforgettable.*

LEFT: *Apparently, swimming with Maui was better than performing at New York's Madison Square Garden.*

THE TRINCOMALEE BLUES – Sri Lanka

RIGHT: *A family outside their bombed house in Trincomalee.*

BELOW: *Fishermen gathering their nets before the nightly curfew: anyone out and about during the twelve hours of darkness is assumed to be up to no good and suffers the consequences.*

RIGHT: *In parts of Sri Lanka, huge numbers of dolphins are captured in nets or harpooned and then sold at fish markets along the coast.*

BELOW: *The blue whale is the largest animal ever to have lived on earth: seeing one in the wild is every whale watcher's dream.*

Duskies have specific bouts of activity, which can be as short as a few minutes or as long as several hours. These include feeding, resting and socialising. If they are feeding or resting they tend to ignore swimmers and approach only briefly for a quick 'hello'. But when they are socialising they are usually fairly playful and indulge in more acrobatics. What we were witnessing may well have been the equivalent of a dolphin disco.

After days in the company of sperm whales, the duskies did not seem particularly large animals. Most of the ones we saw were about six feet long although, out there in the open sea, they seemed considerably smaller. Dark grey above and creamy-white below, they had sleek, streamlined bodies and two 'go-faster' stripes along each side.

As many as 500 duskies spend every summer in Kaikoura, moving close to shore some time in October. The area provides shelter from strong winds, plenty of food and a certain degree of protection from predators such as killer whales and deep-water sharks. The dolphins socialise, feed, breed and nurse their young until the end of April and then, as the southern winter approaches, begin to move offshore and break up into smaller groups. A lone dusky, however, is a rare sight at any time of the year because they are gregarious creatures by nature and genuinely seem to enjoy each other's company. In fact, they are truly cosmopolitan, and spend a lot of time with other animals too: other whales and dolphins, seals and, given half a chance, people.

Skipper Rick Buurman briefed us while we zipped up our wetsuits and washed out the snorkels and masks. He explained that dusky dolphins get bored very easily and instructed us to slip into the water as quietly as possible but, once in, to make lots of noise and to keep moving: dive below the surface, do the loop-the-loop, kick with both legs together (like the dolphins themselves) and sing UB40 songs. No-one thought to ask why UB40; it all seemed so logical at the time.

I sat on the edge of the boat, with my legs dangling in the water, paused for a few moments to watch an endless stream of dolphins whizzing backwards and forwards, and then slipped over the side. It felt as if someone had dropped an ice cube down my neck, as freezing cold water seeped into the back of the wetsuit. But I adjusted my snorkel and mask and swam a short distance away, then looked down towards the seabed a mile or two below. The visibility was only about 15 feet - but somehow I could *feel* the depth, and it took my breath away as I lay there splayed out on the surface.

For a brief moment I could see the distinctive dark and light bands of a dolphin appear at the edge of visibility, but it soon disappeared. Then three more dolphins suddenly came into view. They gave me such a shock, as they sped past like swimmers in a race, that I almost bit through the mouthpiece of my snorkel. The nearest one was no more than two feet from my mask and if I had been quick enough I could have reached out and touched it.

More dolphins appeared from nowhere, their svelte forms leaping over me, swimming alongside, diving underneath, darting this way and that. It was hard to tell who was more excited, them or me. Even females with their calves came to have a closer look, swimming next to one another and touching flipper to flipper like a mother and child holding hands. There were so many others, appearing and disappearing all the time. They twisted and spiralled next to me and watched as I twisted and spiralled in imitation, before unexpectedly changing direction to try and catch me out. They darted towards me, suddenly appearing on a collision course out of the murk, and then peeled off at a tangent at the last possible moment; if I did not flinch, they came back and tried again.

Once or twice, I had a go at singing. Unfortunately, in all the excitement, I could not remember the words of a single UB40 song. So I experimented with an old Beatles number, Yellow Submarine, which seemed quite appropriate at the time. I think it lost something in the translation, as I bellowed it into my snorkel, but it certainly had the desired effect. The dolphins stopped in their tracks (if, indeed, dolphins can do that). I do not know whether it was my singing, or the song itself (perhaps they had heard it before?) but they stared at me, apparently in disbelief, and then came to have a closer look. I swear I even heard one of them try to join in with a brief whistle and click.

Then something unexpected happened. I had grown accustomed to seeing the slim, light-coloured dolphins whizzing into view and out again, but what I saw out of the corner of my eye was unmistakably bulky and black. And it was coming straight towards me. Assuming the worst, I panicked. Goodness knows what was going through my head at the time, but I came straight out of the water as if I had been fired from a cannon and landed, belly down, on the side of the boat.

Rick looked worried. A few weeks before, one of the other skippers had been with the same school of dolphins when a pod of seven killer whales suddenly appeared out of nowhere. They must have approached from below, and in absolute silence, because they caught everyone by surprise. One second everything was peaceful, with dolphins and people swimming happily together, the next it was a madhouse. The killer whales were in a feeding frenzy but, incredibly, took evasive action to avoid harming any swimmers in their way. No-one saw how many, if any, of the dolphins were caught. It all happened so quickly. But the panic was over in a couple of minutes and the whales disappeared as suddenly and unexpectedly as they had arrived.

My 30-foot killer whale turned out to be a six-foot seal. A New Zealand fur seal, to be exact, and it popped its head out of the water to prove the point. I did not feel embarrassed; I just wanted to dive to the bottom of the canyon and stay there for a while until everyone had forgotten that I ever existed. But Rick was understanding and pushed me back into the sea with a friendly shove.

I opened my eyes underwater and the seal was still there. Sharp-eyed and vigilant, it was floating motionless, staring intently at something well beyond my vision in the depths below. It was rather unnerving and I strained to see what scary sea creature might be approaching this time. After a while the seal relaxed and, with a brief condescending glance in my direction, swam away to begin a hectic game of chase. An unfortunate dolphin happened to be passing and was press-ganged into playing. I doubt if it enjoyed the game as much as the seal did – after all, its tail was being nipped – but it certainly joined in the spirit of the occasion and made a determined dash for freedom.

I saw the seal (presumably the same one) a number of times that morning. Never seeming to tire, it swooped around in the water so swiftly and unpredictably that it moved like a burst balloon. It was intent on chasing anything that moved and, a couple of times, when it was fed up with the dolphins winning every game, even turned on me - and playfully nipped the ends of my flippers.

I spent well over an hour watching all the underwater antics, and frequently joining in. The other swimmers were scattered and spread out, hundreds of yards from the boat in every direction, and each of us had our own private audience of dolphins and, occasionally, were joined by the seal. I could hear some of the people shrieking and cheering, but I was mesmerized, watching and thinking in slow motion. It was breathtaking. All I could think of was: 'there are dolphins all around me, dolphins all around'. Life will never be quite the same again.

2

The Trincomalee Blues

BLUE WHALES IN WAR-TORN SRI LANKA

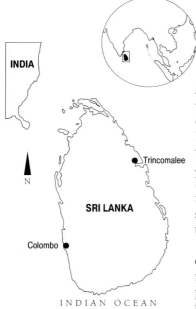

THE BLUE WHALE is the largest animal ever to have lived on earth. It is larger than any of the known dinosaurs. It is almost as long as a Boeing 737 and weighs as much as the entire population of the Falkland Islands (2,000 people). It needs so much food that, in terms of weight, it could eat a fully-grown African elephant every day. A man could hold a party for a dozen friends inside its mouth. It is so large, in fact, that it stretches the imagination and boggles the mind.

Seeing a blue whale in the wild is every whale watcher's dream. But it is a rare animal and, despite its gargantuan proportions, is surprisingly difficult to find. One blue whale has difficulty finding another: for a whale watcher, it is almost impossible. Hundreds of thousands of them were killed by whalers using explosive harpoons, before they received worldwide protection in the 1960s. Nowadays, there are few places in the world where they occur with any regularity and, although there are known to be blues in Sri Lanka, the Sea of Cortez, Monterey Bay, the Gulf of St. Lawrence and Antarctica, even in these places it is possible to spend weeks of searching without seeing a single animal.

I chose to look for them in Sri Lanka. It made an interesting challenge because no-one had been whale watching there for years.

36

In the early 1980s, a small population of blue whales was discovered living off the north-east coast of the island, near a town called Trincomalee. It was actually discovered by accident. Biologists on a research boat, called the *Tulip*, were studying sperm whales in the northern Indian Ocean when they unexpectedly came across a number of blues living in and around Trincomalee Bay. They were able to spend several weeks in the area and counted a total of 35 different whales. It was an exciting find and, almost immediately, local conservation groups began taking people out to see them.

But simmering strife between the Sinhalese people and Tamil separatists exploded at about the same time and the country was plunged into a state of civil war. The troubles continue to this day and, although two-thirds of the island is largely unaffected, Trincomalee is in the troubled one-third and has suffered intense fighting and guerrilla activity for many years. Home to equal numbers of Sinhalese, Tamils and Muslims, it is seen by many as a microcosm of the whole island, but is especially important because of its immense natural harbour. It lies in the heart of a 'no-go' area, which the 'Tamil Tigers' are claiming as an independent state covering most of the north and virtually the whole of the east coast.

There have been several attempts to check on the whales since the *Tulip's* discovery. These were usually under extremely difficult conditions; members of one small expedition, for example, had a narrow escape after their boat came under heavy fire from the shoreline. Plans for further research and, of course, for commercial whale watching, have now been shelved until the fighting subsides.

I travelled to Trincomalee in March 1993 with two friends: Graham Thompson, a fellow whale watcher from England, and Duncan Murrell, a photojournalist based in Colombo, Sri Lanka's capital. Armed with security passes and official letters of introduction, we had just one week – to reach the coast, find the whales and then return to the capital.

It took nearly nine hours to travel 140 miles. The train moved so slowly that, at times, it would have been quicker to walk. It certainly would have been cooler: the overcrowded carriage was like an oven, with the inside temperature rising to 112 degrees Fahrenheit by midday. We stopped at dozens of tiny village stations, each one jammed with new passengers ready to squeeze themselves on board; and, to make matters worse, there were countless unscheduled stops along the way.

There was one particular delay. It was at an abandoned station in the middle of the jungle, the temporary home of about 40 soldiers. Armed with a motley collection of weapons, from pistols to sub-machine guns, they boarded the train and distributed themselves along its length: two in each carriage, one in each doorway. They were our protection, in case of an ambush during the last leg of the journey through Tamil territory.

As it happened, the trip was uneventful. We left the train at a place called China Bay, then followed detailed instructions that had been given to us when we collected our security passes in Colombo:

'When you arrive in China Bay – one stop before Trincomalee – walk out of the railway station and wait for an overcrowded bus, tied together with string and wire, to come screeching round the corner. Stick out a hand and force your way on board. About two miles down the road, leave the bus when you see a dusty track on the left, with a sign saying: 'Do Not Enter. Closed Military Area. Trespassers Will Be Shot Without Warning'. Walk down this track for one and a half miles. Be careful not to step in the jungle undergrowth on either side because the area has not been cleared of mines. After a while, you will see a barrier across the track, with soldiers hiding in a bunker in the woods to your right and in a lookout post on the hill to your left. They will be expecting you. Smile and hand them your security passes, then continue walking for a few hundred yards. You will see some more soldiers, crouched behind a pile of sandbags on the bend, and then the Sea Angler's Club will be visible straight ahead. Walk inside the main building and there will be a man waiting for you with some cold beers.'

The Sea Angler's Club was built in 1965 but looked a hundred years older. Tucked away in the south-west corner of China Bay, a couple of miles away across the water from Trincomalee, it was established (according to the Visitors' Book) 'for people of high standing' and had the air of an old colonial hunting lodge. It consisted of a row of chalets at the back of a tiny beach covered with cuttlefish shells, and a rather ramshackle main building that served as a dining room and bar. In between the two was a path leading to a dilapidated concrete jetty.

Sure enough, there were some cold beers ready and waiting, and we greedily quaffed a bottle each while the bags were whisked away to our respective rooms. We were the first people to stay in the Club for a long time but there was a full complement of staff standing around in the shadows, curiously watching our every move. Strangely, the tables in the dining room were set for 40 people, with half a dozen plastic flowers adding a flourish of colour, although no other visitors were expected. It felt as if we had walked onto the set of an Alfred Hitchcock movie, and were becoming embroiled in a complicated plot that we did not fully understand.

The place was more like a zoo than a Sea Angler's Club – though I have to admit that, with no previous experience of Sea Angler's Clubs, I cannot be entirely sure that they are not all the same. But I doubt it. There were tree frogs under the toilet seats, geckos on the walls, langur monkeys ripping terracotta tiles off the roof, kingfishers perched on the jetty, peacocks calling from the surrounding hills, and kraits in the bedrooms.

A krait is a snake with a rather nasty reputation. Some people call it the 'seven-stepper' because its bite is believed to be so potent that a victim can take only seven steps before dying. It is the serpentine equivalent of a couch-potato, preferring to stay indoors instead of enjoying the fresh air outside. It snuggles up to people in their beds, and then bites them if they have the audacity to roll over in their sleep.

A krait fell on top of me when I pulled back the curtains in my room. It must have been balancing on the rail and, since the chalet had been empty for months, was probably not expecting a roommate. It was hard to tell who was the most shocked. By the time I had leaped back a pace, cartwheeled over the bed and rocketed through the door into the relative safety of the outside world, the frightened snake had dived for cover in a small hole next to the window frame. When I ventured back inside to have a closer look just its tail was visible, waving around in the air.

Kraits in the bedrooms must be a common occurrence at the Sea Angler's Club. Within seconds of hearing the sound of cartwheeling and rocketing through doors, the kitchen staff appeared from nowhere – armed with broomsticks and pieces of bamboo. Unfortunately, it was a rather predictable reaction: snakes are killed on sight in many parts of the world, regardless of the fact that many of them are completely harmless. Even kraits can be placid during the daytime (they become more aggressive at night) and, since this particular one had refrained from biting me, I was determined to let it live. The staff were unhappy about the 'not guilty' verdict, but we agreed to leave the snake alone in the room and I locked the door behind me.

That night I decided to sleep outside. I may be a keen defender of snakes, but I do not like sleeping with them. So I dragged a mattress out to the end of the jetty, rigged up a mosquito net with the help of a rusty old anchor and fell asleep under the most sensational starlit sky.

Less than an hour later, an almighty explosion woke me with a start. I sat bolt upright, the mosquito net wrapped around my head like a giant cobweb, and listened as the explosion was followed by rapid gunfire. It seemed to be coming from a little further around the bay, about half a mile away. I peered across the water, straining to see in the half light of the moon, but there was nothing: no lights, no silhouetted people, no sign of movement.

The sounds of the skirmish continued for more than half an hour. Graham and Duncan joined me on the jetty just as there was a pause and some shouting, then silence. An owl called in the distance and a swarm of mosquitos resumed their infernal buzzing around our ears. We stared at one another in disbelief.

The next morning we were woken unexpectedly by a bugle call at 5.30 am, and rose early for the first recce. A friend of Duncan's had agreed to lend us his boat. He would have lent us his plane as well, had it not been blown up by the Tamil Tigers a few days before.

It was an old wooden fishing boat, about 30 feet long, and was utterly impractical for whale watching. The engine was so noisy that we found it impossible to hold a conversation on board: our voices grew hoarse from shouting to one another above the din. It would have been quieter in a rowing boat, with a Sea King helicopter hovering ten feet overhead. Worse still, the whole vessel juddered so much that it felt as if we were sitting on the lid of a giant food mixer. My camera bag spent all day bouncing around the deck and I spent all day worrying about it bouncing around the deck.

The skipper thought it was hilarious. For some reason, he was utterly miserable most of the time, and looked happy only when we were miserable too. We asked him why, but he just shrugged his shoulders.

To add insult to injury, his boat was called the *Marlin*, after one of the fastest fish in the sea. But its top speed was less than 5 miles per hour and it seemed to take the best part of a blue whale's lifetime to reach the harbour entrance. It should have been called the *Sea Slug*.

Despite our misgivings, we were full of enthusiasm and optimism. Experts from the Fauna International Trust and the Indian Ocean Marine Affairs Cooperation, both based in Colombo, had shown us photographs of blue whales swimming along the coast – within sight and sound of Trincomalee. We had read descriptions of them just outside the harbour and had been told of a place called Swami Rock which was ideal for watching them from the shore. We fully expected to be with the animals by mid-morning, at the latest.

But whale watching is rarely that simple. Our information was based on a small number of sightings nearly a decade earlier and the whales, it seemed, had moved house. We hugged the coast and juddered our way 12 miles north to a lagoon just beyond a place called Nilaveli, but failed to find a single spout along the way. There were no dolphins, either, and few seabirds. In fact, there seemed to be little sign of life at all.

As we approached the lagoon entrance, to take a closer look, we were stopped by a Navy patrol boat. There were almost as many Navy boats in the area as fishing boats, although this was the first one to investigate our activities. Under the circumstances our white skin, the array of camera bags spread out over the deck, and our binoculars, must have looked highly suspicious and, as the boat came alongside, we found ourselves staring straight into the barrel of a sub-machine gun.

One of the men asked what we were doing, and we tried to explain. The Sinhalese word for 'whale' is 'talmaha' but it invariably invoked a blank response and, in this case, my accompanying 'whoosh' somehow made them think we were looking for rockets. It simply added to the tension. We tried charades but the Navy men were getting impatient and we were probably looking more like mercenaries by the minute. Then I went to take a book from my camera bag, wanting to show them a picture of a whale. It was a careless thing to do: the man with the sub-machine gun stiffened and the others went for their pistols. I froze, until everyone loosened up a little, and tried again. This time I moved more slowly, pulling the book out to show them the whale on the cover. It did the trick and there were smiles all round.

But they left us with a warning: we were in Tamil territory and the Tigers were taking pot-shots at boats travelling too close to the shore; seven fishermen had been killed in recent weeks. They waited while we swung our boat around and headed out to sea.

Our skipper looked more shaken than we did and, with an audible sigh of relief, began the long, juddering journey back to Trincomalee. Then he told us why he was so unhappy. He had already experienced the power of the Tamil Tigers at first hand, in a bomb blast a few years before, and he did not want another close encounter. His body was covered in scars and he insisted that we touch a particularly nasty-looking one on his stomach (it felt as if there was a piece of shrapnel still inside, like the blunt blade of a Swiss army knife). I think he wanted us to realise the severity of the situation. Even in war, there can be a semblance of normal daily life and it was all too easy for us naively to lull ourselves into a false sense of security.

The return journey took the best part of the afternoon. We stayed a safe four miles offshore and, by the time we arrived back at the Sea Angler's Club, estimated that we had surveyed nearly 100 square miles of sea. But there was still no sign of the whales, and we were beginning to wonder where to look next.

The following morning we decided to head south but, once again, we were turned back: the Tigers had just taken possession of a small island a couple of miles away, beyond Foul Point. It was inadvisable to get too close.

So we spent the next few hours flagging down fishermen, on their way to the fish market at Trincomalee, in the vague hope that one of them might have encountered a whale during the night.

By lunchtime, we were none the wiser. They were all friendly and tried to be helpful but their comments were baffling and contradictory: the whales have not been around for years; they were here in January; they will be here in five months time; you have just missed them; look further north; look further south; they are ten miles out to sea; they are normally close to the shore; they are at least 20 hours away to the east; they are a day's journey away to the west.

Perhaps we were being optimistic. It was rather like stopping people on the streets of London and asking if they had seen a Harley-Davidson recently. Unless they happened to be motorcycle enthusiasts, most passers-by could be run over by one without actually realising the significance. So it was a bit much for us to expect the fishermen to have been looking out for whales. But we were rapidly running out of ideas and, rather than waste the afternoon with more fruitless questioning, we had a brief conflab and decided to have one more search before dark.

Then it rained. It was the first rain in Trincomalee for three months and the torrential downpour was clearly making up for lost time. The sky was a veil of angry grey and the driving rain so loud that it challenged the noise of the *Sea Slug*. Even the sea joined in the furore, with a heavy swell and breakers making it impossible to tell a whale spout from a whitecap. We decided to turn back.

There was a curfew every night, from 6.00pm until 6.00am. There were no exceptions - walkers, cyclists, rickshaws, cars, buses and boats all had to be out of sight during those twelve hours of darkness. Anyone ignoring the rule was assumed to be up to no good, and suffered the consequences. So we were effectively held prisoner within the compound of the Sea Angler's Club and, by first light each morning, felt a desperate need to get out and do something constructive.

On the third day, we arranged for a motorised rickshaw to take us into Trincomalee. We were ready to try almost anything, and guessed that the fish market might hold a few clues.

A quarter of a mile from the Club we stumbled upon an army patrol of about 30 men, checking the track for mines that were sometimes planted by Tamil Tigers during the night. They made a thorough search first thing every morning. This made us feel secure and in safe hands –

until our rickshaw driver overtook them and, with gay abandon, sped down the unchecked track towards the road. We screeched onto the relative safety of the tarmac, sweating slightly but pleasantly surprised to discover that we were still alive, and continued the journey with a half-hour drive along the shores of China Bay into town.

Trincomalee was smaller than I had expected. It looked a mess, with crumbled buildings wrecked by bomb damage and gunfire. There were soldiers everywhere: standing by the side of the road, peering over the top of sandbag bunkers and manning umpteen roadblocks from one end of the town to the other.

The roads were crowded with people and cattle. There were few cars, and the ones we saw were all Morris Minors. They looked as if they were ready to collapse in a heap of rubble at a moment's notice, but had probably looked like that since the late 1940s and would still look the same in 20 years' time.

We stopped outside what was left of the Trincomalee Hotel. It had been destroyed by a bomb concealed in a pumpkin a month before, and part of the sign - now reading just 'CO HOTEL' - was left hanging by one corner from a broken pillar. The area was bustling with fishermen, busily unloading the night's catch and hauling it into the market across the street. We strolled through the crowd, stepping over giant tuna, paraw, thresher sharks and a host of other fish laid out on the ground, and watched the buying and selling in progress.

Desperately keen to help, our rickshaw driver had been accosting everyone within earshot to ask about whales. He seemed to be entrenched in a lively conversation with three fishermen and, after a while, beckoned us over. In Sri Lanka, people attract your attention by blowing a convoluted kiss which, fortunately, makes a sound more like an irate gecko than a passionate friend. It is their way of saying 'Oi!'. We obediently joined the four men and followed them through the market and out onto a narrow street that led down to a beach.

Lying in the sand was a dead spinner dolphin. It was a young one that, apparently, had drowned in their net the previous night. It was a beautifully streamlined creature with a long beak and an erect triangular dorsal fin. Spinner dolphins are tremendously variable in size, colour and shape and this particular one had a rather distinctive white belly and throat.

In parts of Sri Lanka, huge numbers of dolphins are stabbed to death with long harpoons or caught accidentally in fishing nets, and sold at fish markets all along the coast. The massacre goes on largely unchecked and, while their fins end up as delicacies in Japan, the meat is sold in Sri Lanka as fish. So we asked the fishermen if they had brought this particular dolphin back to sell. They seemed horrified by the idea and, rather unconvincingly, told us that the few dolphins they catch are simply thrown away. But it seemed strange not to throw them overboard, rather than going to all the trouble of bringing them ashore, and we were suspicious.

The dolphin was hurriedly taken away and we tried to explain that we were also interested in 'big dolphin fish', which was a term they seemed to understand. One of the men dived into a nearby hut – presumably his house – and reappeared with a broad smile and two enormous bones. Measuring nearly four feet long, and with distinctive tooth sockets along their length, they were the two halves of a sperm whale's lower jaw. The fisherman explained that the animal had washed ashore several years ago and asked if we wanted to buy some of its teeth. We declined but, with growing excitement, said that we would like to see some living whales instead. He nodded vigorously and drew a map in the sand, pointing to a broad area some distance out to sea. There were whales there. He would take us tomorrow.

We agreed a fee and arranged to meet at his boat early the next morning. At last, we seemed to be making progress.

The trip was a complete disaster. We were duped into spending the entire time watching our hosts fish for tuna and, despite our cajolings and pleadings, did not even get close to the whale grounds that the fisherman had drawn in the sand the day before. We zig-zagged our way out to sea and, every time the boat stumbled upon a feeding frenzy of gulls and terns, towed long fishing lines through the water underneath. Short of a mutiny, there was nothing we could do but sulk, and let our blood pressures rise with the frustration of yet another day lost. It was only when we were back on shore – and refused to pay any money until we had actually seen a whale – that we seemed to have a mutual understanding. We all agreed to try again the following day. It was to be our last day before we had to return to Colombo.

It was already hot by the time we arrived at the boat, early the next morning. It must have been more than 100 degrees Fahrenheit in the shade or, at least, it would have been if there had been any shade. The 35-foot fishing boat was open to the elements and the sun was intense. We were caked in sticky white sunblock and, with wet towels wrapped around our heads and dark glasses protecting our eyes, were a constant source of amusement to the hardy fisherman and his crew.

There was a heavy swell, but with barely a cloud in the sky and no sign of rain we could hardly grumble. The engine was as quiet as a home generator, the camera bag stayed more or less in the same place on deck and we were moving considerably faster than the *Sea Slug* had ever moved in its life. There was a general sense of good things to come as we settled back on a pile of fishing nets for the long journey out to sea.

A small group of about 40 common dolphins joined us for a while, riding our bow wave, chasing us from behind, leaping into the air and racing one another like competition swimmers. But after a few minutes of intense activity they disappeared so suddenly and unexpectedly that we had no idea where they went. They simply dived and we never saw them again.

We were 15 miles north of Trincomalee, and seven miles offshore, when Graham suddenly spotted a blow. It was almost too good to be true. We were all caught off-guard and scrambled to our feet, watching in stunned silence as the whale blew again. At first, after everything the fishermen had told us, we assumed that it must be a sperm whale, which has a low, bushy blow angled forward and to the left. But this blow was slender and vertical in the windless air – and must have been 20-25 feet tall. It was a blue whale.

Suddenly, everything seemed to happen at once. We grabbed our cameras and binoculars, threw our wet towels and sunglasses onto the deck and gave the fishermen frantic directions for a closer approach. There was another blow as we turned, and a few seconds later the whale threw its gigantic tail high into the air and silently disappeared from sight.

We were ecstatic. We clapped and cheered, shook hands, hopped and skipped around the deck and slapped one another on the back. We had seen a blue whale. We had actually seen a blue whale. Even the fishermen seemed happy, especially after checking that they would, after all, be paid in full.

No sooner had we recovered from the initial surprise than another blow broke the horizon to our left. Then there was a second, further out to sea, and a third a couple of hundred yards off the bow. There were whales all around us and, by turning full circle on the deck, it was possible to see up to half a dozen of them in a single sweep. In fact, it was hard to know where to look next, let alone which whales to investigate more closely – a welcome dilemma after all the doubts and frustrations of the previous few days.

The dilemma was almost a hypothetical one because the fishermen wanted to turn back: mission, they thought, accomplished. But when they saw the wild and disgusted looks on our faces, in response, they quickly changed their minds. Every time the whales temporarily disappeared from view, though, they grinned and risked a quick 'OK? Go home?' but on each occasion we managed to squeeze an extra few minutes into the schedule – 10 minutes here, 20 minutes there – until we had satisfactorily re-negotiated the entire afternoon.

Some of the blows were considerably smaller than the first one we had seen. They belonged to Bryde's whales which, unlike most other large members of the family, do not migrate long distances but spend all their lives in tropical and warm temperate waters. They are fairly well known in the Indian Ocean and had previously been recorded off the coast of Sri Lanka by the *Tulip* in the early 1980s. They were usually alone. On a few occasions we saw two or more swimming together but, although they occasionally crossed paths, they barely seemed to acknowledge one another. They reminded me of commuters pointedly ignoring everyone around them as they shuffle onto a train.

We estimated that there were at least 11 Bryde's whales within a small area of three or four square miles. Most were too busy feeding to take much notice of us, although one or two were rather curious and could not resist a brief swim alongside the boat to take a closer look. I have rarely seen whales so active. They were diving and resurfacing every few minutes, changing direction from left to right and then back again, suddenly accelerating or slowing down and generally darting about all over the place. Constantly on the move, and with their prominent, falcate dorsal fins, they sometimes looked more like dolphins than 17-ton whales.

It just went to prove how deceptive size can be at sea. Estimating the length of any wild animal is difficult, but the problem with whales is that they never stay still long enough to be measured and, besides, they show only a small part of their bodies above the surface at any one time. This is why most whale statistics are based on dead animals that have been washed ashore or killed by whalers.

We estimated the Bryde's whales to be about five or six feet longer than our fishing boat, making them about 40 feet. But they were completely dwarfed by their larger relatives, the blues. We saw one blue whale which was considerably more than twice the length of the boat and probably measured 85 feet or more. Perhaps in all the excitement, swirling around on the waves, we overestimated. But even this length is small compared to the longest blue whale on record - an astounding 110-foot female, which was killed in the Antarctic in 1909.

Like the Bryde's whales, 'our' blues also appeared to be feeding. We came across their bright red defecations floating on the surface – a good indication that they were eating tiny shrimp-like crustaceans. These are no more than a couple of inches long, so the whales have to swallow millions of them every day to quell their voracious appetites. Incredibly, the largest animal in the world survives by eating one of the smallest.

We considered getting into the water to watch the blue whales in action, but there was still a heavy swell and it was almost impossible to tell where they would appear from one moment to the next. So we just imagined them, hidden from view beneath the boat, lunging through swarms of crustaceans with their mouths wide open and scooping up huge quantities of their unlikely prey.

When a whale was swimming near the boat, sometimes no more than 50 feet away, its blow was so loud and powerful that it reminded us of the explosions we had heard in the jungle a few nights before. We could almost *feel* the tremendous pressure being released, like a giant cork being fired from a gargantuan champagne bottle. After the blow, an enormous head would appear briefly at the surface; it was undisputably gigantic, even with nothing else in the sea to compare it with. Next came a mottled blue-grey back that seemed to continue forever, as if moving in slow motion. We rarely saw the tiny dorsal fin, which lies towards the end of the back, until the whale was ready to dive. Then the huge tail, which can be an astonishing 20 feet across, was lifted high into the air and, in one flowing movement, slipped silently beneath the waves.

If the sun was at the right angle, we could sometimes just detect the mammoth shape disappearing from view underwater. And then the whale was gone. On the surface, there was barely a ripple and nothing more than a giant flukeprint to prove that we had not imagined such a phenomenal sight. The whole experience was like a dream.

We spent the rest of the afternoon moving from whale to whale, trying to photograph a total of six different blues that we had identified in the area. It was difficult. The cameras were continually being soaked by saltwater spray, we were thrown around the deck by a never-ending procession of angry waves and our eyes were stinging and streaming with tears as they filled with suntan lotion and sweat.

But we had a fair amount of luck with three particular individuals. Two were always together, sometimes almost rubbing shoulders, and they frequently swam alongside the boat. The third was one we took a particular liking to: it was always rather hesitant and, although rarely far from the others, seemed to be something of an outsider. It was never quite able to summon up enough confidence to go over and actually join them. But it posed beautifully for the cameras and lifted its flukes high into the air every time it embarked on a dive.

After nearly three hours, exhausted but exhilarated, we succumbed to a final 'OK? Go home?' from the fishermen and dragged ourselves away. It was just dark by the time we arrived at the Sea Angler's Club and, in an instant, we were back in another, less exciting, world of curfews and kraits.

Blazing Paddles

KAYAKING WITH GREY WHALES IN MEXICO

L A PAZ IS A LARGE TOWN with a small-town atmosphere. Many of its buildings retain their old Spanish colonial charm and the streets are shaded by coconut palms and Indian laurels. Hidden away near the south-eastern tip of Baja California, in Mexico, it sits on a narrow shelf of land overlooking the Sea of Cortez. The Tropic of Cancer is just 50 miles away, across a range of barren hills to the south.

La Paz was the initial meeting place for a week-long whale watching trip, by kayak, along the wild Pacific coast of Baja. I had been told to wait at the Hotel Los Arcos, for a briefing, and arrived to find most of the other 'turistas' and three sun-tanned guides milling around in the lobby.

There were introductions all round, before we adjourned to the bar, ordered some beers and began discussing the trip. We were the kind of mixed bunch that you meet only in the most outlandish places. Among my fellow travellers were two lawyers, an interior decorator, a sports coach, an accountant, an eight-year old schoolboy and Nigel, a surgeon from Halifax. Nigel was one of those people who would have liked nothing more than a complex medical emergency during the trip, requiring delicate surgery in a makeshift field operating theatre. (Fortunately, as it happened, no-one needed delicate surgery, although

48

Nigel himself came quite close to it a couple of times, which would rather have defeated the object).

Steve Smith, the senior guide and a Canadian with many years of kayaking experience, pulled out several well-worn maps and spread them out on the table. With the rusty blade of an old penknife, he traced our proposed route down the coast. The blade pointed to a small fishing village called La Poza Grande, on the Pacific side of the Baja peninsula, which was to be our drop-off point at noon the following day. Then it edged its way southwards, through a string of exotic-looking lagoons along the coast, and eventually stopped at a small town called Puerto Adolfo Lopez Mateos, which was to be our pick-up point a week later. The two settlements were about 60 miles apart and Steve needed three long maps to show us the entire journey. My arms began to ache in anticipation of all the paddling to come.

Steve had done similar trips many times before, but was finding it hard to contain his excitement. He had a broad smile and laughed a lot as he described all the wildlife and places we might see during the week and talked about some of his own kayaking experiences in other parts of the world. His enthusiasm was infectious and we spent a very happy evening poring over the maps, and discussing tents, mangroves, paddles, pelicans, driftwood, guacamole, cameras and whales.

For many centuries, grey whales have made an annual pilgrimage from their rich feeding grounds in the icy waters off Alaska to their breeding grounds in the warm coastal lagoons of Baja California. They gather in their thousands down Mexico way, to court and mate and to give birth to calves conceived the previous year. But to get there requires a 12,000-mile round-trip that takes them along the entire west coast of North America. This is one of the longest migrations of any living mammal and, in a grey whale's typical lifetime of nearly 40 years, is equivalent to a trip to the Moon and back. Just the thought of such a long journey made our 60-mile kayaking trip seem positively feeble by comparison. But we were not there to break records. Our plan was simply to paddle through the sheltered breeding lagoons, taking plenty of time to watch the whales and any other wildlife we found along the way.

During the course of the evening, it became obvious that all the other members of the group were experienced kayakers. Most of their holidays seemed to involve kayaking in one form or another and every time Steve mentioned things like round-bilged hulls, centres of rotation or sweep strokes they seemed to know what he was talking about. Even Thomas, the eight-year old, was experienced compared to me and, in between knowing nods at Steve, chuckled with delight every time I asked an inane question. I was beginning to feel seriously unprepared and cursed myself for not knowing one end of a kayak from the other and for booking the holiday too late to begin the fitness regime that had been so strongly recommended beforehand.

We each signed a form promising never to sue anyone about anything, no matter what happened, and went to bed.

The next morning we were up early and busily packing the mini-bus well before first light. It was rather like trying to seat a family of four and their dog on a moped. We packed and unpacked and then packed again until all our paraphernalia was carefully stowed on board. By the time we had finished, there were six two-man kayaks piled on top of one another on the roof, 13 people piled on top of one another on the seats and a jumble of kitbags, camping equipment, water containers and a week's worth of food squeezed into every nook and cranny that was left.

It was a 200-mile journey north to La Poza Grande. For four hours we trundled along a dry and dusty desert road, stopping occasionally to stretch our legs or to examine some of the extraordinary cacti that littered the undulating landscape in every direction. There was little sign of life, other than turkey vultures sitting by the roadside, a couple of red-tailed hawks flying overhead and an occasional lopsided pick-up truck that passed us by on the other side. We did see a rickety old bus, but it had died in the middle of the road some years before.

Desert is a major part of this wild and rather desolate peninsula. But Baja California is also home to mountains, plains and some of the most impressive beaches in the world, disguising the fact that it grew up harder and lonelier than other parts of Mexico. It has been largely ignored by the 20th century and, outside a few major towns, is thinly settled. Ask why so much of the land is uninhabited and the answer is simple: 'no hay agua', there is no water.

Baja separated from 'mainland' Mexico about 25 million years ago and began moving west at a rate geologists estimate to be about an inch a year. It is now 450 miles away from the rest of the country and has become one of the longest peninsulas in the world, stretching all the way from the Californian border to the town of Cabo San Lucas, more than 800 miles to the south. On a map it looks rather emaciated, varying in width from just 30 to 145 miles, and flanked on either side by the warm waters of the Sea of Cortez and the cool waters of the North Pacific.

We turned left down a sandy track and began bouncing and bumping our way towards the coast. We were driving over a confusion of potholes, rocks and sandbanks that seemed determined to turn our top-heavy vehicle over on its side and, since we were determined *not* to let it turn over on its side, we took more than an hour to travel the few miles from the main road to the end of the track.

We were way behind schedule but, as we lurched into La Poza Grande, could not resist a brief stop. The houses around us were little more than a few boards of wood nailed or tied together, yet each had the most enormous satellite dish strapped to its roof. Some of the glinting, modern dishes were as big as the huts themselves, as if a place to live came free with every satellite dish purchased.

On the other side of the village was a beautiful deserted lagoon fringed with mangroves and we parked the bus on a sandy beach at the water's edge. There were three ospreys circling overhead, their whistled *kyew, kyew* calls echoing across the water as we unloaded the mountain of gear and spread it out on the sand around our feet.

Steve gave us a brief refresher course in sea kayaking, starting (mainly for my benefit) with 'this is a kayak' and adding more detail as the lesson progressed.

Apparently, a kayak is a sub-species of canoe. You sit inside instead of kneeling and use a double paddle instead of a single one. We were using two-man fibreglass 'Tofino' kayaks, which were designed especially for use on the sea and for ease of handling. Each was about 20 feet long, with two tiny cockpits and several interesting extras: elasticated spray covers, a rudder controlled by a temperamental system of ropes and foot pedals, and a simple mast and sails in case we encountered wind.

For the second time that day we started packing. Each kayak had to carry a tent, two kit bags, cameras and binoculars, a couple of sleeping bags, the mast and sails, cooking equipment, enough food for two people for a week, and plenty of water - gallons and gallons of water. It also had to carry the two people themselves, although it seemed unlikely that there would be enough room.

Yet again, I began to feel rather inadequate. Everyone else had arrived with brand new super-tough waterproof bags: I fancied Robin Knox-Johnston may have used similar bags to keep his gear dry while sailing single-handedly around the world. But all I had were some dustbin liners, grabbed from underneath the kitchen sink as an afterthought just before leaving for the airport. Everyone else's gear sat nonchalantly inside their special bags, ready to be strapped in with special super-tough buckles, while mine was stuffed inside the black plastic and tied up with string. I was pleased with myself for remembering to bring string, but vowed to be even better organised next time around.

After the last items had been coerced behind the seats, or strapped onto the deck, we carried each kayak down to the water's edge. They were so heavy I was convinced they would sink but, miraculously, they floated even after we had squeezed ourselves in as well. We said our goodbyes to Scott, a trainee guide who would be driving the bus south to meet us at the other end, watched a flight of pelicans glide past inches above the surface of the water and pushed off into the late afternoon sun.

Three days and more than 30 miles later, we were entering whale country. We had paddled through mangrove creeks and past beautifully sculpted sand dunes, tugged and pulled our kayaks across shallow sandbars and each evening watched the sun setting over the Pacific. It felt as if we had been travelling together for years.

We were moseying along at a steady pace, spread out across a wide lagoon in search of somewhere to camp for the night. Steve was ahead of the main group, peering through gaps in the mangroves and stretching to scrutinise the lie of the land beyond. He was much more at home in a kayak than out and had great style with his paddling. He used long, wide strokes, keeping his paddles shallow in the water, and then paused for a brief moment before his arms moved from one side to the other. It looked so effortless, yet he could move through the water faster than anyone.

Suddenly, he stopped and turned. Waving at the rest of us to slow down, and grinning widely under his sombrero, he gestured towards a couple of round boulders several hundred yards ahead. The boulders moved slightly and then spouted, their far-off plumes rising and falling in the windless air. It was a female grey whale and her calf, resting at the surface.

We caught up with Steve and, talking in excited whispers, agreed to paddle slowly towards them. They were in a 'boca', the gap between two sandbars connecting a lagoon with the open ocean, and as we approached we could see the waves of the Pacific crashing in the distance behind. After a while, we stopped paddling and allowed the hidden currents of the boca to carry us the rest of the way.

The female was a colossal animal. She was at least twice the length of the kayaks, or about 40 feet, and probably weighed in excess of 25 tons. But lying near the surface of the water, with a portion of her back just visible, she still looked suspiciously like a boulder and I would not have been surprised if a pelican had flown along and landed on top. Her slate-grey skin looked velvety smooth, although it was heavily mottled with a variety of white, yellow and orange patches and rings (caused by whale lice) and hundreds upon hundreds of barnacles (a large grey whale may carry several hundred pounds of these small parasites embedded in its skin). The calf was much darker in colour and, as far as we could tell, considerably less than half her length.

The two whales dropped out of sight and left us milling around on the surface. I suddenly felt a little exposed, not knowing whether they were directly underneath the kayak or far away, swimming across to the other side of the lagoon. Everyone seemed to feel the same way and we all stared into the murky water, contemplating their next move.

It was several minutes before they reappeared. This time the female surfaced so unexpectedly – and with such a loud explosion of breath - that we almost leaped out of our cockpits. She was right in the middle of our milling group. Her calf popped up a moment later, still by her side, and no more than ten feet from the end of my paddle. They *had* been underneath us, after all.

During their time in the Baja lagoons, grey whale calves rarely venture far from their mothers. With Mum around they know they are safe: the females have strong protective instincts and, if they feel their youngsters are threatened, can make dangerous adversaries. Yankee whalers nicknamed them 'devilfish' because they used to chase the whaling boats, lift them out of the water like big rubber ducks, overturn them and dash them to pieces with a single stroke of their tails.

But our female whale, somehow aware that we meant no harm, was as friendly and trusting as a kitten. Having inspected the underside of the kayaks, she decided to check on top. Grey whales are believed to have reasonable vision in the air as well as underwater and, in the shallow lagoons, they can 'stand' on the bottom to have a good look around. Sometimes they turn slowly to scan the horizon. There was a slight swishing noise underneath the boats and, suddenly, her enormous, bowed head appeared out of the water. For a brief moment, the tip of her nose was almost ten feet in the air and she was towering above us. I could just make out an eye, staring back, before she dropped out of sight. Clearly satisfied with what she saw, she resumed the boulder position and continued with her rest.

Meanwhile, the calf had no idea what was going on and looked rather bemused. It hesitated for a moment, then rested its chin on its mother's back and settled down as if waiting to see what would happen next.

It was getting late and the fading light caught us by surprise. The Mexican sun seemed to drop like a stone behind the sand dunes and the orange glow of a glorious sunset suddenly turned to darkness. We found a small gap in the mangroves, hauled our kayaks ashore and set up camp in the moonlight. The two whales stayed with us all night. They lolloped in the tranquil waters of the lagoon nearby and, while we were lying in our sleeping bags in the sand, lulled us to sleep with their rhythmic blows. That night, there was nowhere in the world I would rather have been.

We camped on the sandbars every night, with a sheltered lagoon on one side and the pounding surf of the Pacific on the other. Steve was fussy about where we put ashore. At the end of a tiring day, we would eagerly follow him towards a gap in the mangroves, anticipating a rest for our aching arms and dreaming of a sip of smooth Mexican beer, when he would suddenly change his mind and paddle back into the centre of the lagoon for another long stint, until a more suitable gap appeared. They all looked the same to me but, whether by luck or judgement, I have to admit we ended up in some fabulous places.

Once the kayaks were safely ashore, the first task was to unpack. Everyone else pulled out their super-tough waterproof bags, laid their belongings in neat piles on the sand and changed into something warm and dry. I pulled out my torn dustbin liners from the pool of water that inevitably sloshed around in the bottom of the hull, rigged up a washing line between the mangroves, wrung the worst of the water from my clothes and hung them out for the night. When there was enough of a breeze to keep off the dew, they were almost dry by morning and then the heat of the sun would finish the process while I was wearing them the following day.

Next we put up the tents. We had North Face tents which, with a little practice, almost erected themselves. The poles were the key to success, or failure. If you managed to hold them in the right position, and then pushed in a certain way, the tents would rise of their own accord. If you held them in the wrong position, and pushed in the wrong way, they would spring into the air and poke your eyes out.

I was sharing a tent with Nigel, whose main item of equipment was a plastic measuring jug. He used it variously for eating all his meals, for drinking beer and coffee, for measuring nightly rainfall and, while we were out on the water, for having a pee in his cockpit. So I spent as many nights as I could sleeping outside, under the stars. Fortunately, the sand made a comfortable bed and, after all, the incandescent cloud of the Milky Way was a more congenial ceiling than the canvas of the tent.

Unpacked, tents erected and sleeping bags unfurled, we gathered driftwood to make a campfire and sat around, drinking beer, to watch it roar into life. We spent hours around the fire, discussing the events of the day and listening to the sounds of the night: the crackling of the flames, coyotes calling along the beach, a peculiar snapping from the mangroves, an occasional whimbrel disturbed at its roost, the crashing of distant waves and, if we were lucky, the blows of nearby whales. There was so much to absorb and remember, so many sights, sounds and smells that, at times, everyone felt a little overwhelmed by it all and we were often strangely melancholic.

One night, we camped on a sandbar called Isla Santo Domingo. We had eaten a good supper of guacamole, refried beans, tortillas with cheese, spicy enchiladas and burritos and were sitting around the fire, sipping hot black coffee laced with Tequila. The scene around us was surrealistic, with the sand dunes making humped shadows in the moonlight, and we decided to walk across the island to have a look at the other side.

We washed up quickly, in the muddy water around the mangrove roots, put the rest of the food out of reach of thieving coyotes, and set off on the quarter-mile walk towards the Pacific. We could hear the breakers (disappointingly, rather like the hum of a distant road) but could barely see them until we clambered through a series of dunes and spilled out onto the wide, sandy beach below. The blue light of the Moon was enough to see every detail, as if there were special floodlights for night-time strolling.

As we walked towards the southern tip of the island, near the entrance to the boca, we could see a dark shape in the sand. Our worst fears were confirmed as we approached closer: it was a grey whale calf, washed up and dead. Although only a few weeks old, it was 17 feet long and looked enormous laid out in front of us.

Rather naively, our first thought was that the calf might be one we had seen that same day but, on closer inspection, it clearly had been there for some time. Its skin was burned by the heat of the sun and the vultures had already been busy on its lifeless body. We could find no clues to explain its death. Several species of large sharks, including great whites, are abundant in the lagoons, but there were no visible shark bites. Killer whales feed on the tongues of grey whales and then leave them to die, but its tongue was intact. There were no other injuries that we could find and no sign of it having drowned in a fisherman's net. We soon ran out of theories and returned to camp in sombre mood.

Each morning, after a hearty breakfast of scrambled egg, tortilla, porridge, coffee and mango juice, we bumped and clanged in the darkness trying to pack up camp. The tents had to be taken down, the waterproof bags and dustbin liners were filled, and then everything was lugged down to the water's edge. We soon learned that packing carefully first thing in the morning saved futile searches for essential items of equipment (such as chocolate) later in the day, but there was rarely enough time to stop and think. We were in a race against the sun: the best kayaking was in the cool air that lingered for an hour or two before dawn. After that, the sun's rays beat down relentlessly and it was uncomfortably hot until late afternoon.

I have no idea exactly what time we started getting ready. On the first day, at Steve's suggestion, I had taken off my watch and hidden it deep inside my rucksack. It stayed there for the entire trip. I used my biological clock, instead, and went to bed when I felt tired, woke up when the air started smelling of breakfast and, in between, took time cues from the light, my aching arms and hunger pangs in my stomach. It worked surprisingly well.

Clearing the campsite and loading up the kayaks was a real chore. Everything was covered in sand, nothing seemed to fit back into the space it had occupied the previous night and we were always in such a rush. But our moods changed when, after a quick check for litter, we finally slid our kayaks into the water and took the first strokes into a calm day.

The lagoons were magical places of tidal pools, open water, golden sandbanks and mangrove creeks. Exploring them in the kayaks was a delight. We travelled single-file along channels that only kayaks could enter and spread out six abreast whenever we were in the open.

Our paddles barely made a splash and, if necessary, the entire group could move along in almost total silence. It was perfect for watching wildlife. We managed to approach many different birds quite closely and had some marvellous views of night herons and tricoloured herons, snowy egrets, double-crested cormorants, American oystercatchers and many other species.

Brown pelicans were our constant companions. They would fly past in sullen procession, looking as if they had important business to attend to, but going nowhere in particular. They normally travelled in single-file, beak to tail feather. They would flap their wings a few times to rise five or six feet in the air, then rest until a split second before crashing into the sea and suddenly beat their wings again to repeat the whole process. Silhouetted against the morning sky, their heavy wingbeats and enormous beaks made them look like pterodactyls left over from prehistory.

One day, we came across a huge flock of these entertaining birds standing on a sandbar, with a few Hermann's gulls wandering around at their feet. As we paddled by, we noticed half a dozen American white pelicans standing to one side of the main group. Every time one of the white birds wandered over to join the others, it was chased away with a barrage of unfriendly threats and bill-clapping: birds of a feather not quite flocking together.

We were often escorted on our travels by bottlenose dolphins. Their dark, shark-like dorsal fins would appear out of nowhere and, within seconds, there would be seven or eight of the animals playing alongside our kayaks. They were friendly and inquisitive, and sometimes followed us for miles, but always kept a respectful distance. Sometimes they seemed to spend as much time in the air as underwater, turning somersaults, twisting, jumping and, occasionally, lifting their heads above the surface. One particular group stayed alongside for the best part of an afternoon, watched us set up camp and then patrolled up and down the beach until well after dark. We fully expected to see them still there the next morning, but they had gone.

That same night, we camped on the end of a sandbar, near the entrance to a boca, and spent a restless night in the company of twelve Californian sealions. We had seen many sealions during the week, but none quite as memorable as these.

Before our intrusion they had been lying peacefully in the water, their dark chocolate-brown bodies floating on the surface and their flippers poking into the air. Bunched together, in absurdly twisted and contorted positions, they were reminiscent of a kelp bed at low tide. But as soon as we were on dry land, they came to life and clambered onto the beach below the campsite, watching intently as we struggled with the tents and prepared the fire.

They were large animals, a little over eight feet long, and had the raised foreheads that are typical of males. Like a group of friends in the pub, they were commenting on our activities and, as the evening wore on, became increasingly vocal. By the time we settled down for the night, they were so animated and argumentative that we had to shout to be heard above the cacophony of their groaning barks. The din continued until morning. They finally lost their nerve when we staggered out of our sleeping bags and tents, tired and agitated, and shouted at them crossly. In one thunderous movement, they elbowed their way down the beach, dived into the water and disappeared, never to be seen again.

The best whale watching came on the last day. We entered the northern end of Magdalena Bay, approaching Adolfo Lopez Mateos, and could see the distinctive heart-shaped blows of whales all over the lagoon.

There was one whale which swam from kayak to kayak, with the tip of its snout just visible above the water. It seemed to be engrossed in a private game that involved swimming as close to the kayaks as possible, without actually tipping them over. Friendly greys occasionally nudge boats with such enthusiasm that passengers have been knocked overboard, but this particular whale seemed to be well aware of its own strength. There was just one heart-stopping moment, when it surfaced so close to our kayak that its back touched the hull. As we tried to keep balance, Nigel nearly dropped his camera overboard and came dangerously close to turning us over in the process. Then the whale resurfaced on the other side and we were showered in its salty breath (which had exactly the same effect on the camera as dropping it overboard would have had in the first place).

With the animal's head just a few feet away, I found myself staring right inside its blowhole - which is two holes, in fact, each about the size of a rabbit burrow - and felt strangely embarrassed. It was like staring up someone's nostrils and I was so overwhelmed by the experience that I forgot to take a photograph.

That final day really whet my appetite and, when the rest of the group returned to La Paz, I said my goodbyes and stayed behind for some extra time with the whales.

There were no hotels in Adolfo Lopez Mateos, but I met a kindly old man who allowed me to sleep in his chicken shed. It was smelly and baking hot - and the chickens loitered outside every night complaining about the intrusion and discussing the folly of animal rights. Save the whales, but what about the chickens? The shed, however, served its purpose, and I could sit happily in the doorway watching the whales through my binoculars.

There were no kayaks in town either, which was good because I had a sudden craving for a normal boat with an outboard engine instead of paddles. I had enjoyed the kayaking tremendously and it seemed to have little, if any, effect on the whales. But I wanted to take pictures - and kayaking and photography are not a particularly happy mix.

One problem was that my hands were constantly wet: by the time we arrived in the village, all my fingers had turned a light blue colour and they were horribly wrinkled, as if I had been lying in the bath for a week. Another problem was the basic difficulty of manoeuvring the kayak with one hand and taking photographs with the other, especially when a partner in the second cockpit was attempting exactly the same trick. But the main handicap was the fact that my camera bag was stuffed between my knees, which meant that the equipment was virtually inaccessible and my legs were fast asleep for most of the trip. For me to get a picture, the whales had to do something interesting as a kind of preamble, wait patiently until I was ready for a second attempt, and then do it all over again. They never really got it right.

In Adolfo Lopez Mateos the local fishermen have established a whale watching cooperative. They take people out in their boats, on a rota system, and it seemed like an ideal opportunity to do some serious photography.

I particularly wanted a shot of a whale breaching, when three quarters of its body bursts out of the water. I had seen several breaches from the doorway of the chicken shed and, on each occasion, the whale performed two or three times in succession. All I had to do was to find a whale in breaching mood, move a little closer, get ready, and catch it on the third attempt.

But, as is usually the case with wildlife photography, the theory was one thing but putting it into practice was quite another. Imagine hanging around in a rowing boat in the middle of a village pond, with a friend who cannot sit still. Camera at the ready, you are waiting for a fish to jump. You know there are plenty of fish in the pond, but there is no way of telling which one is likely to jump, where it is going to jump, or when it will feel in the mood. After a long wait of several days, you see three separate jumps all in the space of about an hour. One is too far away, the second coincides with a change of film and the third is perfect in every way except for your friend's sudden twitching and jiving, which turns an otherwise good picture into a blurred and lopsided one. It was just like that with the whales. And the boatman was a record-breaking fidget.

In many ways, the calves were easier to photograph than the adults. They were more trusting and inquisitive and, compared to the ones we had seen further north, were less inclined to hang onto their mothers' apron strings. I did not see a calf breach, but they were surprisingly active in other ways.

One day, I watched several of them in the main channel of the lagoon, swimming into the strong current of an incoming tide. They were hardly moving, but struggled against the flow with impressive determination. I discovered much later that the current was like a 'whale gym', and the calves were effectively working out. They were in rigorous training for the long and arduous migration back to their feeding grounds off the coast of Alaska.

It was mid-February and some whales had left their lagoons already. The first animals to leave are normally the males and non-breeding females. Research has shown that they probably navigate using the contours of the seabed, the earth's magnetic field, the movement of the sun, ocean currents and even the different tastes of rivers and bays along the way. With short-cuts (swimming point-to-point across bays and bights) their journey takes about 100 days.

Females with calves leave a couple of months later, giving the youngsters more time to build up their strength and to develop thick, protective layers of blubber to keep out the arctic cold. The calves drink gallons and gallons of their mothers' nutritious milk every day and continue suckling at least until they arrive in the northern feeding grounds. Their demanding journey can take as long as 120 days.

Hugging the Mexican, American and Canadian coastlines, sometimes no more than 50 yards from shore, the whales are watched by devoted whale watchers all along the way. Their migration has become the basis of a major industry, attracting hundreds of thousands of tourists every year: they are probably the most-watched whales in the world.

The first people to take an interest in grey whales were American and European whalers. As the stocks of bowhead, right, humpback and other whales became depleted, they turned increasingly to greys to make their money. By the mid-19th century, they were hunting them in Mexico and from some 15 whaling stations along the North American coast.

Within a few years, so many had been killed that the grey whale was virtually extinct. Charles Melville Scammon, the sea captain who stumbled upon their secret breeding grounds in Baja, must have wondered what he had done when he wrote in 1875: 'The mammoth bones of the California grey lie bleaching on the shores of those silvery waters, and are scattered along the broken coasts from Siberia to the Gulf of California [the Sea of Cortez]; and ere long it may be questioned whether this mammal will not be numbered among the extinct species of the Pacific'.

But, somehow, a small number survived. They received complete protection in 1946 and, since then, have grown in number to more than 20,000. The population is still increasing and, some experts believe, may well be approaching pre-hunting levels. The remarkable recovery of the grey whale has become one of the world's great conservation success stories.

Several weeks after kayaking with the whales in Baja, I was aboard a spacious triple-decked ship watching the same animals migrate past the coast of Los Angeles, in California. They were on the first leg of their journey north.

The ship was one of the largest whale watching vessels in the world. It was 127 feet long, with open-air and glass-enclosed viewing decks, lounge areas, snack bars and room for 700 passengers. It also had two TV rooms: one happened to be showing Daffy Duck cartoons and the other a film on the techniques of downhill skiing; between them, they kept a couple of hundred people amused for most of the trip. Everyone else was outside photographing one another, trying to find lost children, drinking coffee, eating doughnuts and occasionally looking out for whales.

We headed north towards Malibu. A full-time spotter plane had radioed the captain with information on two whales that were further up the coast, and the plan was to go and look for them.

On the way, about nine miles up the coast from Long Beach, we came across a humpback whale. As we approached, it did the most spectacular breach and, in a split second, made hundreds of friends for life. People who had been watching Daffy Duck and the skiing film, below deck, spent the next hour complaining that no-one had warned them something exciting might happen. Everyone else spent it discussing who had managed to get a picture of the magic moment.

With the help of volunteers from the Cabrillo Marine Museum and the American Cetacean Society, who accompany every trip and provide an informative commentary, we found the grey whales without too much trouble. But by the time we arrived, there were five other commercial whale watching boats already with them, plus a small speedboat and two yachts. I estimated a total of 1,700 whale watchers - watching just two whales.

In the past, there have been cases where more than 30 boats have trailed behind just one or two whales along this stretch of the Californian coast. And despite federal guidelines and heavy penalties for harassing the animals, some boat operators navigate much too close and local experts are increasingly concerned for the whales' safety.

But these two animals seemed surprisingly unperturbed by all the attention and continued working their way steadily up the coast. We stayed a sensible distance away, keeping parallel to them at a speed of about four miles an hour, and were able to watch them on their travels for some time.

We found more whales later in the morning, working their way in ones, twos and threes towards their feeding grounds – still several thousand miles away. There were many more laborious weeks of travelling ahead for them.

Then we saw a whale going the wrong way. All the others were heading north, but this one was swimming south. There are a few latecomers every year, but this straggler seemed particularly tardy and barely noticed its contemporaries passing in the other direction. It was either a carefree whale or a badly organised one. But one thing was for sure: it was a whale I could relate to, the kind that would have its belongings packed in a dustbin liner instead of a super-tough waterproof bag.

4

Kujira!

BRYDE'S WHALES AND EX-WHALERS IN JAPAN

N^{O-ONE BELIEVED ME} when I said I was going whale watching in Japan. It must have seemed about as likely as scuba diving in Nepal or downhill skiing in Holland. The only whales the Japanese are supposed to like are dead ones, cut up into a million bite-sized pieces and served as whale sukiyaki or raw whale sashimi.

Two million whales have been slaughtered around the world so far this century and, as a result, some species are now on the verge of extinction. An indefinite international ban on commercial whaling was agreed several years ago to try to reverse the disastrous trend but, in open defiance of world public opinion, Japan neatly sidesteps the issue with the help of a loophole that allows any number of whales to be killed for scientific research. This is nothing more than a sham. There is already enough information on dead whales, but far too little on the numbers, social behaviour, migrations and many other aspects of live ones. Predictably, all the 'scientific' whale meat ends up in rich Japanese stomachs.

Several hundred whales are still being killed every year by the remnants of Japan's once mighty whaling fleet, which has now been consolidated into a four-ship contingent. Minke whales are their quarry. These are the smallest of all the great whales, but they are the only ones that have survived in sufficient numbers to be of any commercial interest.

Whaling is an unbelievably cruel business: there is no humane way to do it. The whalers use barbaric explosive harpoons which inflict appalling injuries, and rarely kill the animals outright. It takes up to an hour for a harpooned whale to die – an hour of intense pain and terror. In fact, the whalers have admitted in the past that, if whales could scream, their industry would have been forced to stop long ago.

But those silent calls for help are never heard above the sound of Japanese money changing hands. Commercial whaling is all about profit. A small number of people are killing whales, and trading in whale meat – despite the cruelty involved and against the wishes of millions of people around the world – for no better reason than to line their own pockets. The dockside value of a single, ten-ton minke whale is around £30,000 and, once in a Tokyo department store, its meat can sell for more than £100 per pound.

But there is a glimmer of hope. A growing army of more recent converts to the whales' cause may have found an answer to the problem: they are determined to change Japan from a nation of whale hunters to a nation of whale watchers.

The country's first whale watching trip left Tokyo, in April 1988, bound for the Ogasawara Islands, more than 600 miles to the south. Despite tremendous opposition from both whalers and government officials, a small, pioneering group of whale watchers spent four days enthralled by the local singing and breaching humpbacks. They returned home fired with enthusiasm and their close encounters made TV and newspaper headlines across the length and breadth of the country.

The trip was a sensational success and marked a crucial turning point for Japan. During the months that followed, the whale watching phenomenon began to spread: first to Cape Muroto, then Ogata and then to four other towns and villages up and down the country. Now several more coastal communities are planning to follow their lead and, almost overnight, Japanese whale watching has become big business. In 1992 alone, some 20,000 people paid nearly half a million pounds to watch whales in Japan, bringing in total revenues (including travel, food and accommodation) of an incredible £5 million. There have been many free trips as well – for schoolchildren, students and local people – in a determined effort to demonstrate that whales look better than they taste.

Japan now has one of the fastest-growing whale watching industries in the world and, if the trend continues, it will not be long before live whales really are worth more than dead ones. When that happens, even the most stubborn and mercenary Japanese whalers will be hard pushed to argue a case for killing them.

I have an admission to make. I never really wanted to go to Japan. Its track record on the environment hovers on the verge of international vandalism and has always rather clouded my view of the country. Whaling, driftnet fishing, the ruthless exploitation of tropical rainforests and many other issues formed an impenetrable smoke-screen in my mind. For many years, I was never really inspired to look behind the screen and thought of Japan as little more than a murky, something-to-do-with-the-Japanese place somewhere in the distant Far East. I had a mental image of workaholic salarymen, loyal workers chanting company anthems, bus-loads of camera-toting tourists, subservient women, and of strange men in boxer shorts crawling through tunnels full of earthworms for TV game shows.

Having now been to Japan I am none the wiser. My prejudices have not really changed, although they are certainly more complicated. I encountered a kaleidoscope of contrasts and contradictions at almost every turn: ancient history rubbing shoulders with ultra-modern; staggering beauty suddenly giving way to concrete ugliness; and traditional values and customs colliding with modern-day hustle and bustle. The people were especially perplexing: polite and friendly one minute, aloof and uninterested the next; thinking as individuals yet behaving instinctively as a group; and profoundly spiritual yet so materialistic that their true religion seems to be shopping.

Tokyo was the most baffling city I have ever visited. It is a huge, sprawling place that would take a lifetime to explore properly, so my two-day recce of the central districts may have been misleading. But, unlike many other capital cities around the world, it is less a collection of noteworthy buildings and points of interest than an overall experience. More than anything else, the sheer level of energy is indelibly stamped on my memory: crowds of people surging through the streets and a barrage of noise and flashing lights assaulting them day and night. There is so much activity and movement that nothing – except the traffic – seems to stand still. There are incredible laser shows between the skyscrapers; miniature TV screens built into traffic lights; electronic voices talking at passers-by from shops and banks; vending machines playing dreadful Japanese pop songs; and colossal three-tier roads and monorails vying for air space in the skies above. Arriving there was like travelling forward in time: it felt as if I had landed somewhere in the middle of the next century.

By the end of the second day, I was still wrestling with a riddle of confused impressions. I did not understand Tokyo at all. Every time I thought I was beginning to get a feel for the place, something totally

BLAZING PADDLES –
Mexico

ABOVE: *A grey whale just finishing its impersonation of a boulder: notice the distinctive series of 'knuckles' in place of a dorsal fin.*

RIGHT: *In their shallow breeding lagoons, grey whales can 'stand' on the bottom and lift their heads above the surface to have a good look around.*

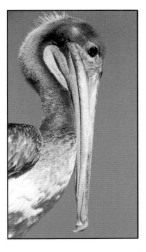

LEFT: *Brown pelicans were our constant companions; their heavy wingbeats and enormous beaks made them look like pterodactyls left over from prehistory.*

ABOVE: *One particular whale seemed to be engrossed in a private game that involved swimming as close to the kayaks as possible, without actually tipping them over.*

LEFT: *Coyote tracks in the sand; we spent every evening sitting around the campfire, listening to the high-pitched yapping of coyotes along the shore.*

RIGHT: *We were often escorted by bottlenose dolphins; friendly and inquisitive, they sometimes followed us for miles but always kept a respectful distance.*

LEFT: *As we walked towards the dark shape in the sand, our worst fears were confirmed: it was a grey whale calf, washed up and dead.*

BELOW: *A grey whale's tail, photographed from the doorway of a chicken shed.*

BELOW: *Sunset signalled a rest for our aching arms, time for a bottle of smooth Mexican beer and another peaceful night sleeping under the stars.*

RIGHT: *Nagaoka Tomohisa, ex-whaler turned whale watcher, scans the horizon with his binoculars firmly wedged onto the end of a short bamboo pole.*

ABOVE: *A Risso's dolphin looking as if it has been dragged through a thorn bush backwards.*

BELOW: *One of the few pictures of a Bryde's whale I managed to take without a bright red Japanese hand-bag dominating the frame.*

ABOVE: *This whale had a strange, mottled appearance caused by circular scars all over its body, as if it had had a particularly severe dose of chicken pox.*

LEFT: *Japan has one of the fastest-growing whale watching industries in the world: it may not be long before live whales are worth more than dead ones.*

ABOVE: *Cape Muroto is easy to find on a map, but surprisingly difficult to find in real life.*

THE SNORKEL PARTY –
Canary Islands

RIGHT: *A whale's eye-view of whale watchers.*

LEFT: *If I were a whale living off the coast of Tenerife, I would seriously consider moving somewhere else.*

ABOVE: *Over 500 different short-finned pilot whales have been identified off the coast of Tenerife and there is a photographic record of them all.*

BELOW: *Underwater, the pilot whales reminded me of pedestrians walking past a drunk in the street: some hurried past, pretending not to notice, others snatched a quick glance and then carried on their way, but a few paused to have a blatantly good stare.*

RIGHT: *Some of Tenerife's pilot whales are true Canarians and live there throughout the year, others stay for just a few weeks or a few months, and the remainder, like many of the more sensible human tourists, visit briefly and never return.*

RIGHT: *Like icebergs, pilot whales normally show little of themselves at the surface; but this one is spyhopping, providing a brief glimpse of its distinctive rounded forehead .*

BELOW: *A 'Whale Safari' is high on the must-do list for many visitors to Tenerife.*

unexpected happened. I finally gave up when I started seeing grown men wandering around a region of the city known as Shinjuku in their pyjamas.

But while Tokyo represents everything that is brash, new and high-tech in Japan, to leave the relentless pace of the city is to step into another world. It is like travelling backward in time. Cape Muroto is such a place: a wild and rugged finger of land, in south-western Japan. Jutting into the North Pacific, it is the home of some 24,000 people, a chain of black, sandy beaches and a busy little harbour; a battered white lighthouse, perched high on its wildest clifftop, overlooks the town.

Muroto is easy to find on a map (look for the sharpest point on the fourth largest island) but surprisingly difficult to find in real life. Few people outside the main cities speak English and, since the Japanese writing system is one of the most complex in the world, road signs and public transport timetables are a monumental challenge. For a *gaijin* (a foreigner or, literally, an 'outside person') travelling in Japan is confusing at the best of times. Travelling to Muroto, which is well off the beaten track, is about as confusing as it gets.

I was warned not to hire a car (the indecipherable signs ensure that foreigners in cars are rarely seen again) so was travelling by bus. Knowing when to get off was the main problem, especially with a sense of direction as fallible as mine. As we trundled down the coast road from Kochi City, stopping to swap passengers every few miles, I checked each sign we passed on the basis that, eventually, one would match the script for 'Cape Muroto'. I knew exactly what I was looking for because I had memorised it. As far as I could tell, the town's name consisted of three distinct characters: a dalek, an upside-down saucepan wearing a hat, and a peregrine falcon swooping past a waffle on a stick. My script analysis skills almost worked and, after nearly three hours on the road and just two false disembarkations, the bus stopped for the umpteenth time and I was physically pushed off by the driver.

I was in Muroto to meet a remarkable man: ex-whaler turned whale watcher, Nagaoka Tomohisa. Nagaoka has spent nearly half his life killing whales. He began in 1950, working from small boats and with hand-held harpoons off the Cape Muroto coast. For several years he hunted the animals as local fishermen had done for centuries. Then he became a professional harpooner and spent nearly 20 years patrolling Antarctic waters aboard a commercial whaling ship. Among the respected elite of the industry in Japan, he won awards for some of the largest catches on record and was widely acclaimed as one of the country's best harpooners. Astonishingly, he killed more than 4,000 whales during his long career.

I did not expect to like Nagaoka, despite his recent change of heart. But he was a delightful man, a fit and healthy 61-year old, with closely-cropped grey hair, enormous fisherman's hands and a kindly smile. He was seriously deaf after years of working the harpoon gun.

We met at his house and talked through an interpreter. In its heyday, he told me, whaling was a prestigious occupation. While he was with the whaling fleets at the bottom of the world, spending up to six months at a time on long trips away from home, local schoolchildren used to send him letters of encouragement and parcels of food. He freely admits that he enjoyed the work and he earned good money; whaling, he says, paid for his son's education. (There were photographs of his son, vying for wall space with pictures of whales, in virtually every room of the house; a major celebrity in Japan, and Nagaoka's pride and joy, he became a high-ranking sumo wrestler, with the ring name Asashio, and is now the sumo stable master Wakamatsu. His father gave me a blow-by-blow account of each picture of the mean-looking, monster-sized Asashio in action).

After his retirement, in 1978, Nagaoka became a bonito fisherman. But he missed the whaling days – not the killing, he told me, but the excitement of the Antarctic expeditions and, more importantly, the company of the whales themselves. Since Muroto was full of ex-whalers, he had resigned himself to evenings spent reminiscing with old friends.

Then, in 1989, he was asked by the local government to study the potential of whale watching as a way of boosting the local tourist industry. After all, who better than an ex-whaler to do the job? Nagaoka was enthralled by the idea and, with the help of two old whaling friends (Chiyooka Yoshinobu, another retired harpooner, and Yamada Katsutoshi, a former whaling ship officer), he carefully surveyed the surrounding seas. The three men soon discovered that the Cape Muroto area was brimming with whales and dolphins. Risso's and bottlenose dolphins, sperm whales and short-finned pilot whales were all living within sight of the town and so many other species were present in smaller numbers, or sometimes passed through, that it was impossible to know what was going to turn up from one day to the next. Muroto was a whale watcher's paradise.

Nagaoka had no hesitation in setting up his own whale watching company and, by the time I arrived in town, just four years later, he had already taken more than 7,500 people out on his boat.

It was dark when we finished talking, so we arranged to meet again early the next morning and I walked back along the coast to my minshuku. A minshuku is a traditional Japanese inn. Staying in one is a good way to peep into daily Japanese life, but it can also be a nerve-wracking experience for unwary Westerners still struggling with rigid Japanese social etiquette. There are so many potential *faux pas* that you feel strikingly conspicuous and clueless throughout your stay. You must bow whenever you meet people ('treat everyone like the King or Queen of

England', someone told me); try not to fill every silence in a conversation with words; never blow your nose in public (it is admirable to sniff) and try to sneeze quietly (even if you have a cold); do not stick your chopsticks upright in the rice (that is how it is offered to the dead); and, most important of all, always wear the right slippers.

There is a range of uncomfortable plastic slippers for every occasion in Japan. Learning which ones to wear, and when to wear them, is an important strategy for survival. Only a *gaijin* would be careless enough to get it wrong; even Japanese burglars have been known to remove their shoes and don the appropriate slippers before entering a house for a quick burgle.

You put on the first pair before passing over the threshold. There is usually a selection of different sizes lined up at the doorway, from small to extremely small; none are even remotely large enough for a flipper-footed foreigner. Then you change slippers again (or go barefoot – I never did work out which to do when) before entering certain rooms, such as the dining room or bedroom, and before strolling around the garden or wandering around town. Toilets have their own special, brightly-coloured slippers which are instantly recognisable; these are the cause of intense embarrassment if you forget to change them after a visit. The first time I made the mistake all the other guests made me feel as if I had sprouted extra limbs, though everyone did see the funny side when I proffered unintelligible noises of apology.

The next morning, safely back in normal shoes, I walked to Sakihama Port, just north of Muroto, and found a small group of Japanese tourists milling around Nagaoka's boat, the *Suehiro-maru II*. There was a businessman from Kyoto, a student from Osaka and a young couple on holiday from Hiroshima.

Within a few minutes, Nakaoka himself arrived, wearing a centuries-old sweater and a frown. The weather was bad, he warned us with gross understatement, and we might not be able to find the whales at all. But after a brief discussion in Japanese (which, by default, excluded me) we agreed to have a look anyway. It made a certain amount of sense because at least one of us had flown 10,000 miles specially for the privilege and the others had remembered to bring wet-weather clothing and super-tough waterproof bags for all their gear.

As we left the harbour, the 50-foot fishing boat was rising and falling in the heavy swell. So were the remains of last night's sushi. By the time Muroto was a mere speck in the distance, it was the kind of weather that brought to mind emergency flares, Mayday calls and air-sea rescues. There was a bitterly cold wind blowing offshore, whipping the waves into such a frenzy that it would have been impossible to tell a whale spout from a whitecap. After two miserable hours, Nagaoka suggested that we give up and return to shore. No-one objected.

The next day the weather was even worse and I was the only passenger on board. A small flock of red-necked phalaropes struggled past on whirring wings and we followed them out to the edge of the continental shelf, a few miles offshore. An hour later, the sea had calmed just a little and, with his binoculars firmly wedged onto the end of a short bamboo pole, for stability, Nagaoka scanned the horizon for signs of life.

Self-confessed whale addict, Moritoshi Hamasaki, with one of his friends.

He had barely finished the first scan when a dark, sickle-shaped dorsal fin suddenly appeared almost directly behind the boat. Neither of us really saw it at first, but we seemed to sense its presence at exactly the same time and both yelled out, Nagaoka in Japanese and me in English. Nagaoka swung the wheel and the boat turned around sharply as we raced towards the disappearing shape. I glanced at him. His eyes were shining with excitement and he laughed, embarrassed, as if I had rebuked him for acting like a whaler back on the hunt.

Other fins appeared around the boat, as we stopped, and soon we were surrounded by more than 40 Risso's dolphins. These are strange animals with blunt heads and white scars and scratches all over their bodies. Some of the older ones, which were probably 12 or 13 feet long, had so many scars they looked as if they had been dragged through a thorn bush backwards. Their battered appearance is caused by fights with other Risso's dolphins, although all the members of this group seemed to be relaxed in each other's company.

The dolphins stayed with us for more than an hour. Spread out across a wide area, in small groups of twos, threes, fours and fives, they appeared to be feeding. But one particular member of the school seemed determined to attract our attention. It slapped its tail and flippers onto the surface and, after each dive, briefly popped its head out of the water to check that we had not disappeared. When we finally began to head back towards the shore it suddenly breached, right next to the boat, launching itself high into the air and falling back with a tremendous splash. We did not see it again.

I spent the rest of the week sitting in a small cafe, drinking thick, dark coffee with Nagaoka and complaining about the worsening weather. He probably did not understand a word I was saying, but I could tell that he was just as fed up. Gloom and disappointment travel across the language barrier without the need for lengthy discussion.

A steady trickle of tourists from all over Japan passed through the town, hoping to see whales. But they were invariably turned away with an apologetic word or two and an indignant glance towards the dark, stormy clouds. The wind and rain did stop briefly once and, with a long-awaited nod from Nagaoka, a small group of us scampered down to the boat. In the rapidly fading light, we spent what little was left of the afternoon patrolling backwards and forwards up and down the coast, but to no avail. There were no whales and, this time, there were no dolphins either.

I decided to move on.

Ogata is not so much sleepy as comatose. It reminded me of a small Swiss town which I once had the dubious pleasure of calling home, known as Gland. Both places have neat rows of houses, perfectly tarmaced roads, orderly hedges and ubiquitous black kites wheeling and turning overhead. But there are two important differences. The first is that Gland overlooks Lake Geneva, while Ogata overlooks the North Pacific. The second is that Gland is merely boring, while Ogata is comatose in a soporific and rather appealing way.

As the crow flies (if it were flying straight across Tosa Bay) Ogata is about 80 miles due west of Cape Muroto. It is a long, narrow fishing village, with a small population of around 11,000 people. There is nothing unusual about the village itself, but it is reputed to be the best place in the world to see Bryde's whales. Sixteen of these little-known whales live just offshore, spending most of their time within a few miles of the village, and have spawned a lucrative and rapidly expanding whale watching sideline for the local fishermen.

I checked into another kind of Japanese inn, called a ryokan. This is supposed to be like an upmarket minshuku, but the distinction between the two seemed to be rather fuzzy. An elderly kimono-clad maid showed me to a room which was so small I could barely lie down and, even then, I had to do it diagonally. There was no furniture, other than a miniature, ankle-high wooden table, and the bed consisted of nothing more than a shallow mattress rolled up and squashed into one corner. Even the walls were made with delicate sheets of waxy rice paper, instead of bricks and mortar; one false step and I would have crashed next door into the kitchen, and goodness knows what slippers I would have needed for that.

The room's saving grace was a floor-to-ceiling window overlooking the sea and, as I dropped my bags onto the grass-matted floor, the first thing I noticed was a small group of bottlenose dolphins milling around in the shallows no more than 50 yards away. I liked the place immediately.

Given the chance, I would have ordered a glass of ice-cold beer and watched the dolphins until supper. But it was bath-time. Bathing in Japan is a serious business and absolutely no-one is allowed to be late for such an important ritual.

The bathroom was huge and communal (although men and women were segregated) and was clearly the pride and joy of the inn. There was a rigid procedure to follow, which I found anything but relaxing: take off your clothes in a small hallway and place them in a basket; move into the main bathing area; pull up a stool and bucket; sit down under a tap and have a really good scrub; and then, finally, when you are squeaky clean and well rinsed, you are allowed to sink into the steaming hot water of the bathtub itself. The golden rule is that the tub is always for soaking – never for washing. To scrub and rinse in the bath is unforgivable, akin to farting in a lift or slurping spaghetti.

Perhaps I scrimped on the scrubbing and rushed the rinsing, but I happened to be ready first and had a rather stressful soak while the others waited for me to finish. I kept it as brief as I could, and pulled out the plug. The entire bathroom erupted into a state of panic and confusion. I had no idea what was happening until someone stepped forward, dived into the water between my legs, fumbled for the plug and put it back. The Japanese, it seems, share their bathwater.

Supper was served in a small dining room. I had been told by the maid to wear my dressing gown. But it was still only six o'clock in the evening and I assumed that I must have misunderstood what she was really saying. However, it is wrong to assume anything in Japan – always expect the unexpected – and, sure enough, I was the only guest in normal clothes. I felt as embarrassed as if I had turned up at a restaurant in London with no clothes at all.

There were six of us eating and, since no-one spoke both English and Japanese, we spent the entire meal smiling and nodding at one another. We sat on square cushions on the floor and were served by two waitresses who bowed deeply every time they entered or left the room. It was like trying to eat in the middle of an aerobics class and, by the time we had finished, I had the most terrible indigestion. The food itself did not help. The Japanese diet is supposed to be one of the healthiest and tastiest in the world, but after eating raw egg, raw fish, raw octopus and raw squid for breakfast, lunch and supper every day for over a week, my stomach was beginning to revolt.

Even the whale watching in Ogata included an element of eating: fisherman Moritoshi Hamasaki served up a raw katuo fish at the end of every trip. It was usually one that had been floating around in the oily water in the bottom of his boat, but it was always served in a delicious sweet soy sauce and I have to admit it tasted good.

Hamasaki and his fisherman friends had been struggling to make ends meet when they heard about the pioneering whale watching trip to the Ogasawara Islands. Whale watching was something they had not considered before, but they often used to encounter whales on their fishing trips and were intrigued by the possibility of taking tourists to see them as well. They investigated further and, encouraged by what they found, set up their own whale watching cooperative in 1989. Now there are 44 registered fishing boats, taking people out on a rotational basis according to demand: if one boat is out fishing, the next on the list is called.

In 1992, they had 5,300 customers. Before the end of the decade, the annual figure is expected to rise to 30,000 or more. Whale watching already accounts for a third of the fishermen's annual income and is expected to earn them around £4 million over the next 15 years. It will also generate nearly eight times as much through hotel accommodation, food, travel and other supporting industries. It has become so important for the town that the cooperative now has its own office to handle all the bookings, to advise on local accommodation and to deal with the press. At one time or another, everyone in the town's Fisheries and Commerce Section, which runs the office, has been conscripted to answer endless telephone calls about the whales.

But the most remarkable aspect of the entire industry is that it is based on such a small population of just 16 animals – making each whale worth more than £100,000 a year. To put this into perspective, if all these whales were killed for food (as some people in Japan would undoubtedly prefer) between them they would fetch around £3 million in a fish market. A small number of whalers would get rich very quickly, but they would leave everyone else with nothing to develop for the future. Killing whales, in Ogata at least, no longer makes economic sense.

I was on the water with Hamasaki almost every day. His boat was licensed to carry four people, and was usually full. The other whale watchers were all Japanese and, while many had simply made a detour after noticing whale signs along the main road, or after passing a life-size mural of a Bryde's whale just outside the village, others had travelled long distances specially for the privilege.

I took the opportunity to ask them about whaling, but it was a touchy subject. Their faces clouded the moment the dreaded 'w' word was mentioned. Many people I spoke to were openly unhappy about discussing it with a *gaijin* and several told me, very politely, to mind my own business. One man scowled for several seconds before pointing out that, whatever *anyone* thought, it was a government decision and one that would be made without the influence of foreign pressure; his wife ignored me for the rest of the trip.

It made a difference whether I broached the subject before we set off from the harbour, or after we had returned. It was more fruitful afterwards, though whether this was because everyone trusted me a little more having spent several hours together, or whether it was because they had seen whales for the first time, I do not know. I like to think it was the whales but, whatever the reason, their answers were quite revealing. Most of the youngsters and, surprisingly, many of the older people, were positively *against* killing whales; some had strong views on the subject, others simply felt that whaling was no longer necessary.

One particular family was so bowled over by their first whale watch that they abandoned their touring holiday halfway through and spent the entire second week in Ogata – to go whale watching every single day. And they vowed never to eat whale meat again. I am sure they really meant what they said but, like many Japanese people I had met before them, they may simply have been giving me the answer they thought I wanted to hear.

There was also the problem of Japanese etiquette. I gave everyone a hypothetical situation to ponder: suppose they were at a dinner party, or a business lunch, and their hosts served up whale meat; would they refuse to eat it and risk causing offence? Most people looked at me as if I was completely mad and the answer was inevitably the same: the thought of appearing rude or ungrateful was absolutely out of the question.

I saw my first Bryde's whale from the harbour entrance, less than a quarter of a mile offshore. We idled closer and Hamasaki switched off the engine. A moment later the dark grey whale surfaced no more than a few yards from the boat. Either its curiosity outweighed any fear, or whales forgive and forget more easily than their human friends, because Bryde's whales were systematically hunted off the coast of Japan until quite recently. Ogata's residents have never been commercial whalers but, nevertheless, this particular animal was so friendly and trusting that it made me feel strangely guilty about the atrocities of the past.

As it swam slowly around the boat it seemed completely at ease, despite the hullabaloo on board. An elderly Japanese woman was

A Bryde's whale surfaces next to the boat.

shrieking and yelling and waving her arms in the air with uncontrollable excitement. At one point, she was almost hysterical and ruined a potentially great picture by slapping me on the back just as the whale lifted its head out of the water; when I had the picture developed, some weeks later, it showed a blurred image of her bright red handbag.

The whale was about 40 feet long and had three prominent ridges along the top of its head, running from the blowhole to the end of its snout. These are unique among whales, making the Bryde's relatively easy to identify at close range. But its most striking feature was the dorsal fin, which was so prominent and sharply-pointed that it looked rather like a scythe. I imagined that anyone foolish enough to fall out of the boat, and on top of the whale, would probably have been sliced in half.

As the whale continued its circling, there was a constant crackle of chatter on the radio. The fishermen talked incessantly all day long. They probably discussed everything from women to weather but, unfortunately, I cannot understand crackly short-wave radio conversations when they are in English, let alone in Japanese, so I cannot really be sure. Suddenly, there was a word I *did* recognise – 'Kujira!' – a whale. The voice on the other end was shouting 'Kujira! Kujira! Whooo! Haiii!' and everyone looked up. Hamasaki started the engine. One of the other fishermen had found a whale that was breaching: it had already leapt out of the water several times in a row and was still going strong.

We waited until the whale next to us arched its back and safely disappeared below the surface and then Hamasaki swung the boat around towards the south. It was several minutes before we rounded a small peninsula and saw the other fishing boat. The whale was still there – we could see its powerful blow rising in a tall cloud 10 or 12 feet into the air – but it seemed to have finished breaching. A brief radio message confirmed our disappointment. (Hamasaki wrote to tell me that, soon after my visit, one of Ogata's Bryde's whales breached 70 times in a row and made Japan's television news).

As we came alongside, it was obvious that this whale looked quite unlike the one we had just left. It was still a Bryde's whale, but it was a distinctive chocolate-brown colour instead of a dark grey. It also had a strange, mottled appearance caused by circular scars all over its body, as if it had suffered a particularly severe dose of chicken pox; the scars were probably made by cookie-cutter sharks, which have a nasty habit of hanging on to whales with their lips and then boring out neat plugs of flesh with their razor-sharp teeth. As we watched, a second whale unexpectedly surfaced right next to the boat. Perhaps it had heard the noise of the breaching (which travels a long distance underwater) and had swum over to investigate? It dropped a couple of yards below the surface and lolled in the water for several minutes, apparently oblivious to the row of enthralled faces watching its every move. As we leant over the railings, the first whale drifted towards us and gently rested its chin on the newcomer's back. It was immediately below where we were standing. I held my breath. Even the hysterical woman with waving arms was rendered temporarily speechless. Then, in one flowing movement, the two animals separated and dived. We looked at one another and just shook our heads. For once, language was not a problem: there were no words to describe how we felt.

Hamasaki never tired of whale watching. On several occasions, I am sure he would have stayed out all night if I had not been obliged to rush back for my daily bath. He must have seen the whales thousands of times but his mixed feelings of curiosity, excitement and admiration never waivered. He knew each one personally and, even when he was out on fishing trips, always stopped to greet them. He described it as like bumping into old friends in the street.

With friends like Hamasaki the whales are in with a chance, but the final decision is down to the Japanese Government. The rest of the world is waiting.

The Snorkel Party

SWIMMING WITH PILOT WHALES IN THE CANARY ISLANDS

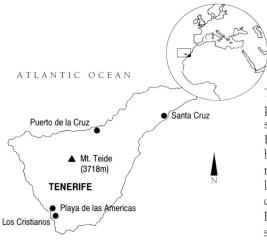

ATLANTIC OCEAN

Puerto de la Cruz

Santa Cruz

▲ Mt. Teide
(3718m)

TENERIFE

● Playa de las Americas
Los Cristianos

N

Playa de las Americas, on the south-west coast of Tenerife, is the archetypal package holiday paradise. Its streets are lined with 'real' English pubs and karaoke bars, all-night discos, pulsing neon lights and staggeringly large hotels. Its beaches are crowded with German and English tourists, vying for sunbeds and fighting for space in the sand.

But even the most well-frequented places still have their secrets, and this particular tourist hot-spot has one of the best: it is home to a resident group of short-finned pilot whales. Several hundred of these little-known members of the dolphin family live just a few miles offshore. Some of them are true Canarians and live there throughout the year, others stay for just a few weeks or a few months, and the remainder, like many of the more sensible human tourists, visit briefly and never return.

Tenerife is the largest of the Spanish-owned Canary Islands, an archipelago of seven main islands lying roughly 900 miles south-west of mainland Spain. The nearest landmass is actually Africa (the coasts of Western Sahara and Morocco are less than 70 miles away) but centuries of Spanish rule have given the Canaries a distinctly European flavour.

With a pleasant climate all-year-round, and cheap flight connections with Northern Europe, they attract more than five million holiday-makers every year. Half these people find their way to Tenerife and, as a result,

76

few parts of the island have been left untouched by tourism. There are still barren deserts, lush green valleys, steep sea cliffs and rugged mountains; there is no denying the splendour of its centrepiece, Mount Teide, an active volcano and the highest peak in all of Spain, which soars out of the Atlantic to a height of 12,600 feet. But much of the natural beauty has been lost to colossal and ever-expanding holiday resorts. The south coast, in particular, is utterly dedicated to mass tourism.

It comes as a shock to find whales of any kind living along such a busy and booming coastline – one of the most touristy corners of the entire archipelago. But it is even more surprising to find pilot whales, since they tend to live in very deep water a long way offshore.

At first glance, Tenerife's pilot whales seem to have made a terrible mistake – but there may be method in their madness. The island provides shelter in the middle of the open sea, and deep, nutrient-rich water right next to the coast, and the area abounds with squid and deep sea fish – the very creatures that pilot whales like to eat.

There are few places in the world with these special conditions. There are even fewer where, as a result, you can expect to see pilot whales so close to shore.

Like icebergs, pilot whales tend to show very little of themselves at the surface. The view from above is quite deceiving – normally little more than a rounded forehead, a low, thick-set dorsal fin and a small part of the back. So, to see them at their best, you have to be prepared to get wet.

Donning snorkel, mask and flippers, I began to lower myself over the side of the boat, a little nervous and unaware that the top step was as slippery as an ice rink. In one continuous movement I lost my balance, crashed my head against the railings and fell backwards into the sea. I surfaced, and turned, just in time to see the last of the whales change direction and the trailing dorsal fin disappear below the surface.

The trouble is that, although pilot whales weigh up to four tons, can grow longer than 20 feet and are built like Sumo wrestlers, they do not like a lot of fuss. It is not good enough simply to *get* into the water – the technique is to *slip* into the water. And to do it quietly.

The skipper yanked me back on board and slowly eased the boat ahead of the whales once again. We travelled in a wide arc, to cause as little disturbance as possible, and then he cut the engine ready for a second attempt. As far as I could tell, there were 18 animals in this particular pod. Swimming parallel to the coast, with the gleaming white hotels and apartment blocks of Playa de las Americas less than two miles away on one side and the open Atlantic Ocean on the other, they were spread out, shoulder-to-shoulder, in a long line. Two huge males were riding shotgun and they were clearly in a lazy mood. For a moment or two, we just listened to their rhythmic breathing as they swam slowly towards us.

I prepared for another sortie and, being a little more careful than before, managed to clamber over the side without incident. This time the whales did not seem to notice, though I am sure they knew I was there: occasionally the victims of sharks, they always have to be on guard.

Floating in the warm water next to the boat, I took my first look under the surface. According to some of the locals, there are hammerheads and blue sharks living in the area – and only a few weeks before, in exactly the same place, a local diver had had a close encounter with a great white shark; apparently, he survived to tell the tale with nothing worse than half a missing flipper and a ripped wetsuit.

I was rather sceptical about the great white shark story but, as a rule, imaginary sharks are much worse than real ones. They are bigger and uglier and generally more dangerous, so when I first peered underwater it was with a panicky glance in every direction. I was breathing in short, sharp gasps and my heart was pumping so fast I thought I might pass out. It took me some time to calm down.

I am embarrassed to admit it now, but I was also a little unsure about the whales themselves. I kept thinking about a home video I had seen on American TV, just a few weeks before. It showed two people swimming with a small group of pilot whales off the coast of Kona, in Hawaii. In full view of the camera, a whale suddenly turned towards one of the swimmers, opened its mouth and bit her on the thigh. She swam away as fast as she could... and then there was a break in the film. The next scene showed the same whale at a depth of 30 or 40 feet, with the woman desperately struggling to release her leg from its jaws. I particularly remember how tiny she looked: she was dwarfed by her attacker. The final part of the encounter was not filmed but, according to the two people involved, the whale seemed to change its mind and simply carried the woman back to the surface. Barring a few stitches, she was apparently none the worse for her experience.

It is impossible to guess what prompted the whale's behaviour. The swimmer herself firmly believes that it was not being aggressive but simply playing a game, albeit with near-fatal consequences. One thing is for certain: it would have had no idea that people are poorly adapted to life underwater; a pilot whale can hold its breath for 15 minutes, and dive to depths of more than 2,000 feet, so it would have been reasonable for it to assume that we can do the same.

I could not get the images of the film out of my mind and letting go of the boat was like cutting an umbilical cord. But I pushed myself away and began to swim, slowly and quietly, towards the line of whales. Looking down towards the seabed, 3,000 feet below, there was nothing but depth in every direction. The sea was a clear, deep blue; and all around me the sun's rays were shining through the surface layers, like hundreds of torch beams.

The plan was to position myself directly in the whales' path and then simply to wait for them to come to me.

I kept checking on their progress and finally, some distance from the boat, stopped to watch the row of fins heading in my direction. They took my breath away. When you are in the water, the sight of approaching fins – no matter what they are attached to – seems to invoke a physiological reaction that starts the adrenalin pumping around your body much faster than normal. The whales looked much bigger than they had done from the safety of the boat and their *staccato* explosions of breath were much louder than I had expected. I did not anticipate any trouble but, at the same time, I had no idea how they were going to react to my intrusion.

For some reason, I had assumed that they were all close to the surface, but when I dipped my head underwater I was shocked to see a female with her calf immediately below me. In the heat of the moment they seemed to be within touching distance, but they were probably 20 or 30 feet away. As I watched, the mother rolled onto her back and swam along upside-down, perhaps to study me more closely. Her calf remained close by her side – so close, in fact, that the two animals seemed to be stuck together with glue.

As they glided out of sight, I realised that, in my excitement, I had been swimming towards them and was now about 10 feet underwater and surrounded by whales. They were all around me, their huge shapes gliding by in ones, twos, threes and fours.

Some were really inquisitive and came to have a closer look, others seemed to be unmoved by this strange person flailing about in their midst. They reminded me of pedestrians walking past a drunk in the street: some hurry past pretending not to notice, others snatch a quick glance and then carry on their way, but a few pause to have a blatantly good stare.

I was sure I could sense a few of them staring and, once, turned around instinctively to find a whale watching me closely from behind. But it was more than a sixth-sense: it was a particular tingling sensation that I had never felt before. Rather like a very mild electric shock, it made the hairs on the back of my neck stand on end and was almost certainly caused by the whale investigating me with its sonar, the focused beams of sound hitting my neck and shoulders and then bouncing back ready for the inquisitive animal to decipher. Pilot whales build up a 'sound picture' of their surroundings by analysing the pulses of sound that bounce back from nearby objects, using a similar system to the one used by bats for 'seeing' in the dark. Their sonar is especially effective, probably as an adaptation for feeding on squid, which are almost acoustically 'transparent'.

I needed to breathe and, as soon as a suitable gap appeared, swam back to the surface. The whales did not seem to be moving very fast, but it was deceptive: a few barely perceptible flicks of their tails and they were gone. The experience had seemed to last a lifetime, but it was probably all over in less than a minute.

I began to swim back towards the boat and was almost there when the unmistakably huge fin of a big male broke the surface of the water directly in front of me. He was no more than a few yards away and, at first, I thought we were going to collide. But just as I put my head underwater, to have a closer look, he moved slightly to my left and began to dive. I dived as well and began to swim alongside.

A pilot whale about to prove that looks can be deceptive.

I was finding it hard to keep up when, without warning, he stopped in mid-water. He appeared to be smiling, but all pilot whales have upturned mouths that make them look mildly amused – and looks can be deceptive. Since I had no idea what he was thinking, I stopped as well. He turned his head towards me, then opened his jaws wide and snapped them shut. They opened so wide, in fact, that his entire head appeared to consist of two equal halves joined together at the back by a hinge; for a brief moment, despite the rather inappropriate comparison, he reminded me of a muppet. He clapped his jaws again, and again, and this time I took it as a warning not to come any closer. Suddenly there was something unnerving about his fixed grin, and about the way he was behaving, so I backed off a little and watched him continue his dive in peace.

Swimming with whales once is not enough. It is more than a simple alternative to watching them on the surface. It is a different experience altogether, heightened by entering their world instead of just standing on the sidelines. It becomes addictive and, while in Tenerife, I was in the water with the pilot whales at every opportunity.

Each time, I knew a little more about what to expect. I was calmer and better able to observe them more closely. Most important of all, I felt I had learned a little about their own criteria for proper behaviour and etiquette and was able to let them decide when enough was enough. I tried not to swim straight towards them, avoided sudden movements and always gave them plenty of space.

Consequently, my early encounter with the jaw-clapping male was the only hint of aggression that I witnessed all week. I felt as if I had an unspoken agreement with the whales: I respected their limits and they allowed me to join them for an occasional swim. I began to recognise individuals, by the shapes of their dorsal fins and distinctive scarring on their bodies, and felt an incredible affinity with them.

It was impossible to tell whether the whales felt any kind of affinity with me, or if they were simply putting up with my presence. Researchers who have swum with them off Tenerife have observed aggressive body language, such as jaw-clapping, bubble-blowing and head-shaking, on many occasions. So it is possible that, once you are experienced at recognising signs of aggression, you notice it much more. Perhaps I missed some of them and have jumped to all the wrong conclusions. I sincerely hope that they were not irritated by my presence, but it is something which has been troubling me since.

I was also strangely troubled by the thought that these close encounters were happening in the Canary Islands, within sight of one of the busiest holiday resorts in Europe. It felt as if something was wrong: somehow, the experience better suited a place like Tahiti, or Fiji, or The Maldives.

Sadly, in many ways, something really *is* wrong. Although Tenerife offers a wonderful opportunity for people and pilot whales to meet, there has been a sudden, money-driven, surge of interest in whale watching that threatens to frighten the animals away from the area altogether.

On the day you arrive in Tenerife, on a package holiday, you are invited for a drink with your holiday company representative. It is an opportunity to get your bearings and to find out what will be happening during the week. The rep briefs you on everything from how to avoid time-share touts (look under 25 and try not to walk around in couples) to drinking the local water.

Unfortunately, the brief does not include a warning about the local whale watchers. Not all of them are to be avoided, of course, but there are some who should never be allowed near a whale again.

Whale watching, Tenerife-style, is a free-for-all. No special permits are required, there are no official guidelines or regulations and there is no governing body to oversee what is happening. Anyone who wants to set up a whale watching operation needs nothing more than a simple licence, similar to one required to take people water skiing or paragliding. After that, they can do more or less as they please. The licence is just a formality and little, if any, consideration is given to the welfare of the whales.

Most of the pilot whales in Tenerife live along a surprisingly short stretch of the south-west coast, typically no more than a few miles offshore. Each day, they seem to make a slow sweep of a small area, following a deep submarine canyon that is formed by the proximity of Tenerife and Gomera, a neighbouring island to the east. It may have been my imagination but, in the mornings, they seemed to hang out together, resting and generally taking life easy. In the afternoons, they split up and became more active until, as the sun began to set, they left the area and headed for even deeper waters offshore. They are believed to feed mainly at night, when squid migrate from great depths towards the surface and are much easier to catch.

In calm weather, usually until mid-afternoon, the whales are easy to find. Anyone with reasonable eyesight can track them down. The whale watching boats simply leave the marina, head directly out to sea and, after 20 minutes or so, start looking for the tell-tale dark shapes in the water. Some do not bother searching at all; instead, they look for other whale watching boats that have already stopped (next to the whales) and go to join them.

In recent years, the number of people taking holiday-makers whale watching has increased dramatically. A trip to see the whales is now high on the 'must do' list of many visitors to southern Tenerife and it seemed to me that almost anyone with a boat was trying to get in on the act. Yet most of the skippers I met had no previous experience of whale watching. Many of them saw the whales as nothing more than a source of income to be exploited, rather than a source of wonder to be treated with respect.

There were home-made placards sprinkled all over Playa de las Americas, advertising all the whale watching tours available, and the operators themselves were constantly touting for business. The placards rarely had company names, just a general heading 'See the Whales and Dolphins' or 'Whale Safari', with some holiday snaps of people sunbathing and drinking beer on a crowded deck, swimmers around a boat and a distant shot of a couple of fins. But they seemed to do the trick and were attracting plenty of business.

All the operators were offering essentially the same product: a sail along the coast, 20 minutes with the whales and an hour anchored off a 'deserted' beach. For most people, the beach seemed to be the highlight of the trip – a chance to have a swim followed by a feast of Spanish omelettes and beer or sangria. Unfortunately, all the whale watching boats tended to storm the beach at the same time, making it anything but deserted. But no-one seemed to mind.

The boat trips themselves were pleasant enough. With sailing time as well, each one lasted for about three hours. Most people sat on the sun-warmed decks, soaking up the rays and enjoying the view of Mount Teide and its spectacular volcanic surroundings. There were plenty of other boats to watch, to pass the time of day, and there were often small schools (or flocks?) of flying fish skimming low over the surface of the water just ahead of the bow.

But for me these 'sun, sea and sangria' trips were ruined by the whales. Not by the whales themselves, of course, but by the trauma of watching them. A few skippers used good common sense and clearly had some respect for their 'quarry'. They approached the animals slowly, kept engine noise to a minimum and then left them alone if other boats appeared on the scene. They were very helpful and keen to please, although I have to say that their knowledge about whales was virtually non-existent. Most were unable to answer the most basic questions (like about the food they eat or why they live off the coast of Tenerife) and one even expressed surprise when he learned that there is more than one kind of whale.

On several occasions, I saw small groups of whales literally surrounded by boats. When this happened, they often lay passively on the surface. It looked as if they were resting and, at first glance, they seemed to be quite undisturbed and relaxed. But studies have shown that many whales are so acoustically sensitive that, when there is too much engine noise underwater, their sonar systems become useless. So the animals are literally trapped by the relentless din around them. We can only guess at the sense of terror they must feel to be forced to shut down completely.

When encountering a single boat, their reaction tended to vary according to their own activities. One afternoon, there was a high swell and we found a single whale surfing in the waves. Like a human surfer, it kicked hard to get ahead of a wave, rode it until there was no strength in the water left, and then turned ready for another go. It was so engrossed in its game, it took no notice of us floating nearby.

But their reaction also varied according to the behaviour of the skippers. Some skippers played loud disco music, which clearly was not a good start. One catamaran I saw, crowded with people drinking beer and messing about on deck, was towing an eight-foot blow-up killer whale behind the boat. Everyone, except me, seemed to think it was an hilarious joke. Somehow, the whole atmosphere took away the magic and the feeling of humility that you get when watching whales in other parts of the world. These people were turning the animals into a source of amusement, and I found it all very difficult to stomach.

I saw several skippers cause the whales to panic. The scared animals would split up and dive, stay underwater for much longer than usual and then reappear in a group some distance from the boat. What did the skippers do next? They turned around and chased them all over again.

One man, in particular, behaved atrociously. He was taking people out on private charters and had an enormous speedboat that he enjoyed pushing to its limits. Time and again, I saw him race up to the whales at such high speed that his wake washed all over them. He chased the bemused animals all over the place and then, when his clients had had enough, opened the throttle and sped back towards the shore; he never gave a second thought to the whales that might have been underneath his boat at the time.

These are not isolated incidents. I happened to witness them during a brief 10-day stay in Tenerife, so it is not hard to imagine how many whales have probably been injured in recent years. There are already reports of whales with damaged dorsal fins and scarred backs, and others with open wounds that were clearly made by boat propellers.

Until proper regulations can be introduced in Tenerife, it is up to the whale watching companies, the tour operators and the whale watchers themselves to regulate the industry and to give the animals a satisfactory level of protection. Individual pressure is the only way to raise awareness and to ensure that the whale watching is safe and considerate.

In the meantime, if I were a whale living off the coast of Tenerife, I would think about moving somewhere else.

A pilot whale, complete with distinctive fin, loitering next to the boat.

One day I was so frustrated with the whale watching 'professionals' that I persuaded one of the skippers to try a different technique. We spotted a huge group of about 30 animals milling around a couple of miles offshore and cut the engine about 50 yards away, just to sit and watch.

After a while, the whales became at least as curious about us as we were about them and, slowly, they made their way over to have a closer look. If whales could amble, that is exactly what they were doing. A young calf was a little braver than the others and swam ahead of the pod, until its mother caught up and gently guided it away. One particularly inquisitive individual lifted itself half out of the water, as if trying to peer inside the cabin, and several others swam upside-down to inspect the hull.

Their curiosity apparently satisfied, they settled down to loiter next to the boat and, at one point, there were six or seven of them on either side. I resisted the temptation to reach out and touch one.

Each whale had a distinctly-shaped dorsal fin. Some were shark-like or triangular, others were sickle-shaped and curled over at the top. One had such a droopy tip that it appeared to be melting in the hot morning sun, and I almost expected to see it dripping. The males had the strangest fins – enormous ones that were especially low and broad-based and leaned backwards as if they had started to collapse.

Every fin also had the animal's personal history engraved on it, in the form of scars, scratches and nicks, making it relatively easy to tell one individual from another. Over 500 different short-finned pilot whales have been identified off the coast of Tenerife since September 1989, and there is a photographic record of them all. Taken by a husband and wife research team, Jim and Sara Heimlich-Boran, the pictures are helping to fill in some important gaps in our knowledge about the whales' day-to-day living arrangements. Until Jim and Sara arrived on the scene, no-one had studied short-finned pilot whales before (other than dead ones) and their private lives were shrouded in mystery.

One recent discovery is that many of the female pilot whales are quite elderly, and can live to a ripe old age of 65 or more. On the face of it, this probably sounds like a rather everyday thing to discover. But it is interesting because, in the wild, most animals die when they reach retirement age. An early death makes a lot of sense. When an animal is too old to breed, and is of little use to the 'community', it is still munching its way through the local food supply – so from everyone else's point of view, the sooner it dies the better.

Female pilot whales, on the other hand, have found an excuse to stay alive for longer. They make themselves useful by caring for their offspring for 20 years or more and by baby-sitting for other females. Like village elders in a traditional human society, they may also pass on their knowledge and experience to other members of the group. So they still have an important role to play.

In contrast, the poor old males have not managed to find an equivalent excuse and, consequently, have a life expectancy of just 45 years.

Some of the animals were lying on their sides, with one flipper and half a fluke sticking unceremoniously out of the water, but most were hovering just below the surface. They were in such a state of languor and keeping such a low profile that, from a distance, they probably looked like floating logs. They were not exactly sleeping. Whales and dolphins probably do not need much sleep and they seem to cat-nap for a few minutes at a time. They never have a long, deep sleep in the same way that we do and, even when they are snoozing, are often still on the move. What happens is that the two halves of their brain work in shifts, with one side shutting down while the other keeps watch. It must be a bit like a guard on sentry duty outside Buckingham Palace, trying to cope with the boredom but keeping a watchful eye on the Queen at the same time.

The whales and I were in a fairly quiet mood when the silence was broken by a sudden commotion in the water, about 100 yards away. I sat bolt upright. If they had been capable. I am sure the whales around the boat would have sat bolt upright too. At first, I thought that one of them was being attacked but, as I watched, a bottlenose dolphin leaped into the air, and then another, and another. There were dolphins all over the place. A group of them had joined us, and they were clearly in a mischievous mood. Their sharper, more professional-looking dorsal fins were slicing through the water in every direction, they were performing high, arc-shaped leaps and they were splashing about like excited children in a paddling pool. It was impossible to tell how many there were – I did not know where to begin counting.

The pilot whales hardly knew what to make of it all. Once they had recovered from the initial shock, they started diving more frequently. Then they began to lift their tails out of the water and slapped them down onto the surface. One or two even tried some rather amateurish leaps themselves. I have no idea whether they welcomed the intrusion, and were joining in all the fun, or whether they were furious about the disturbance and were determined to make their feelings felt.

The dolphins soon tired of their game and disappeared as quickly as they had arrived. I decided to leave the whales alone, as well, and headed back towards the karaoke bars and pulsing neon lights on shore.

I had spent more than an hour with them. I could have stayed a lifetime.

6

Orca Waters

FRIENDLY KILLER WHALES IN CANADA

JOHNSTONE STRAIT

Port Hardy
Telegraph Cove
Campbell River
CANADA
Vancouver Island
Vancouver
Tofino
N
Victoria
PACIFIC OCEAN
USA

Do you remember *The Waltons*, the long-running TV series about an American family living a simple life during the Depression? It was a high point of the 1970s. All the men wore dungarees, and had crinkly necks after too much time in the blazing sun, while the women gossiped with Ike in the General Store.

You may recall that three generations of Waltons lived together. Grandma and Grandpa, Mama and Papa, and the seven grandchildren – John-Boy, Mary-Ellen, Jim-Bob, Jason, Aaron, Ben and Elizabeth – all shared the same rambling wooden house in the shadow of Walton Mountain.

Well, strangely enough, killer whales, or orcas, have been living like the Waltons for thousands of years. Not in rambling wooden houses, of course, but in close-knit family groups. They arrange themselves into discrete units, known as sub-pods, pods, clans and communities, that have a peaceful, Zen-like quality about them. These units bridge the generation gap and are so stable and harmonious that only death, or capture, can break them apart.

The heart of orca society is the mother and, in fact, the maternal bond is so strong that her children never leave home. Even strapping 30-foot, nine-ton grown-up males are tied to their mothers' apron strings for the whole of their lives (the relationship between mother and son is purely filial and not, as was once suspected, incestuous: John-Boy does not mate with Mama but casts his net further afield). This basic family unit, which often includes the grandmother as well, makes a 'sub-pod'.

The Waltons themselves formed one of these sub-pods. But they were unusual because, strictly speaking, Grandpa and Papa should have disappeared from the scene a long time ago. If they had been orcas they would have had nothing more than brief liaisons with Grandma and Mama and then they would have returned to their own sub-pods to continue living with *their* mothers. In real life, this arrangement means that young orcas always come from single-parent families but, on the plus side, they are likely to have several half-brothers and half-sisters to keep them company.

As you might imagine, a 'pod' is composed of several sub-pods. It is an extended family group and consists of a few closely-related mothers (usually sisters or cousins) and all their offspring. It is rather like a family get-together at Christmas, only much more permanent and with none of the fathers and very little of the arguing. One pod is distinguished from another by language or, to be more precise, by dialect; each has its own unique dialect just as we have in human languages.

Pods with similar dialects belong to the same 'clan' and all the clans sharing the same part of an ocean belong to a 'community'. In Walton-speak, a community is roughly equivalent to a nation. There are considerable language barriers between individuals from different communities, just as there are between people from different regions or nations. In all likelihood, a whale from one community would find it hard to chat with a whale from another: it would be akin to a Londoner trying to make himself understood in Glasgow.

If you are not confused by now, there is every chance that you will be very soon. These sub-pods, pods, clans and communities are merely the nuts and bolts of orca society and, in practice, their living arrangements are even more interesting and complicated; in fact, although orcas are among the better studied of all the world's whales, there is still a great deal we have to learn.

Ironically, though, certain individuals are staggeringly well known. Biologists have been studying a number of them for 20 years or more and the animals have become old friends. In particular, the orcas living in British Columbia, Canada, and in Washington State, USA, have been kept under close scrutiny since the early 1970s and are better known than most. More than 300 different whales in the area have been named and numbered and, indeed, many of them have been studied in considerable depth. Sometimes, studying orcas must seem rather like running a private detective agency – every animal has a personal file, containing umpteen mug-shots and an abundance of information on all the finer details of its private life. Some of these files are probably more comprehensive than their human equivalents in the vaults of the CIA, MI5 or the KGB. So if you are an orca living in British Columbia, or Washington State, the chances are that your friendly neighbourhood biologists know everything about you, from your mother's maiden name to your favourite food and a great deal more.

I visited Vancouver Island to find one particular pod, known as A5, which currently contains 14 family members. Twelve of them live wild and free in protected waters off the north-eastern coast of the island. The remaining two – Corky and Yaka – live in marine parks many hundreds of miles away, and are tragically confined to two small concrete tanks.

The surface of the sea was smooth and calm, the sun barely visible through a thin veil of mist that enveloped our boat. A river otter scampered for cover underneath a rock (it occurred to me that the same one had probably been responsible for keeping me awake the night before, chomping on a bony fish head immediately below my bedroom window); a dog barked as we slipped away from the wooden boardwalk and a bald eagle cackled from somewhere overhead. It was a perfect still morning in August.

I was among fellow whale watchers on board a 60-foot vessel called the *Gikumi*. With Bill MacKay at the helm, we motored south into Johnstone Strait and there was a general feeling of good things to come. This narrow stretch of water, sandwiched between Vancouver Island and the rugged coast of mainland British Columbia, is one of the best places in the world to see orcas. A number of pods congregate in the area every year, from late June until early October, to feed on the local salmon. Some have been known to greet the *Gikumi* at the harbour entrance and, in fact, there are so many orcas in Johnstone Strait that, if you do not see one, you may as well give up orca watching and embark on an even more predictable hobby such as train spotting or Morris dancing.

We were lucky. A small pod had been reported in nearby Alert Bay. We drifted out into the Strait and Bill decided to cut the engines and wait. It seemed like a good idea because, with so much mist around, the whales were more likely to find us than we were to find them and, after all, if anyone knew how to secure a close encounter, Bill was our man. He had been out to meet them hundreds, or even thousands, of times - on almost every summer's day since 1980 – and I suspect he felt more like an honorary member of some of the pods than a mere observer.

While we waited, I sat next to a large woman clutching an equally large handbag. She was caked in suntan lotion and talked incessantly. She simply never stopped. First she told me about her pet poodle, then about the time she nearly appeared on the Johnny Carson show and then, for no apparent reason, she started to moan about the problem with gardeners in her home town of Phoenix, Arizona. Poor Phoenix. The next subject was her nosy neighbour and she had just clenched her fist to demonstrate how she planned to deal with him when there was an almighty explosion of breath from inside the drifting mist. There was a second blow, then another, and another, and all of a sudden a sea of dark fins came into view about 50 yards away to the stern. They stopped the woman cold, her clenched fist locked in mid-air next to my chin, and for the first time that morning she stopped talking. Her jaw hung wide open, but the next mouthful of babble was never delivered. I was very impressed by that: four whales and she was completely dumbstruck.

I do not blame her. The fact is that nothing prepares you for the sight of your first pod of orcas. No matter how many times you see them on television, or how often you read about them in books and magazines, in real life they take your breath away. They leave your brain grappling with the improbability that anything so powerful, so beautiful and so graceful could all be rolled into one.

As the four animals emerged from the mist there was an almost ridiculous sense of drama on deck, as if we were witnessing a significant moment in history. All I can say is that it *felt* significant. Only a lump of rock could have remained unmoved by the scene that was unfolding before us. The whales moved purposefully through the water towards the boat: three females and, just half a beat behind, a young calf. The tips of their sickle-shaped dorsal fins broke the surface first, jet black in colour and glinting in the hazy light, then there were brief flashes of white as their heads came into view. After four more blows, they dipped below the surface and, as though moving in slow motion, disappeared underneath the hull.

It was hard to believe that we were in the company of the largest and most powerful predators on Earth. If you believe the sensationalist press, orcas are supposed to be evil, aggressive animals always ready to attack anything that moves. But the truth is that they do not deserve their fearsome reputation. They are no different from other top predators, such as lions, tigers and polar bears, except for one simple fact: they never hunt people. No-one knows why they should make an exception. There is no logical reason. Yet there has only ever been one 'attack' in the wild – and that was on a surfer who survived after the whale realised its mistake and spat him out.

Many people have spent countless hours watching orcas from boats, with no hint of aggression, and others have swum with them and lived to tell the tale. I have been kayaking with them. Two huge males, with their dorsal fins towering nearly six feet above the surface of the water, rode shotgun on either side of me. It took a while to come to terms with their sheer size, of course, but I never felt threatened. Far from it, I sensed an awareness and gentleness that was quite overwhelming.

After a few moments 'our' whales reappeared, this time four abreast on the other side of the boat. They surfaced with a single, united explosion of breath, catching us all by surprise. My cameras were soaked by the spray and the woman from Phoenix had such a shock I thought she would never speak again. Then the four animals paraded along the entire length of the *Gikumi*, like customs officers inspecting a ship before allowing it to dock, and, apparently satisfied, slowly disappeared into the mist.

As everyone regained their composure, there was a buzz of excitement around the deck and Bill identified the whales as belonging to A5 sub-pod, which is part of A5 pod itself. I could not believe my luck. My first encounter was with the very pod I had come to see - and within 48 hours of leaving London. There was Licka, a female born in 1953, her two daughters Havannah and Holly, and Holly's son, Ivy, who was born in 1991. (Ivy turned out to be a male *after* he had been named and will probably be teased as a bit of a 'girlie' for the rest of his life).

Licka's other daughter is Yaka, who was captured and taken into captivity in 1969. The two animals have been separated ever since.

I stayed in the tiny village of Telegraph Cove, which is carved into the rugged coast of Vancouver Island where Johnstone Strait in the south almost meets Queen Charlotte Strait in the north. It is an isolated community, built around a lumber mill and staring across the water towards a chain of breathtaking snow-capped mountains that rise to more than 12,000 feet above sea level. The setting is awesome, like the rugged west coast of Scotland but on a much grander scale – as if it is being projected into a fairground mirror that makes everything seem wider, taller and more distorted.

Telegraph Cove once served as the northern terminus of a telegraph line that was strung from tree to tree along the entire length of the island's rugged east coast. Nowadays, it is better known for its houses, which stand on stilts in and around the harbour and are joined together by an old wooden boardwalk. The village has a year-round population of only about a dozen people, though in the summer it is bustling with campers, fishermen, boaters and, of course, whale watchers. Dozens of people turned up at the village every day, specifically to see the whales. Many of them never wanted to leave. I heard couples discussing it in the car park: 'Well, if we skip the northern part of the island, and do not visit Auntie Gladys, and forget about the beach day for the kids, and then leave for Vancouver at four in the morning on Saturday, we could spend two more days with the whales'. I should have warned them – I stayed for two weeks and it was not nearly long enough; not even close.

My stay in Telegraph Cove was punctuated by orcas and food. One day we identified no fewer than 53 different whales, though I lost count of the number of times we had food. I just remember feeling as though breakfast was followed by elevenses, twelveses, brunch, lunch, high tea, low tea, a three-course dinner and then supper. There were refreshments in between and, on a couple of occasions, when the river otter was keeping me awake, I even squeezed in a midnight snack as well. Eating was always a cue for something interesting to happen and many of the meals were interrupted by rhinoceros auklets, tufted puffins, Steller's sealions, Dall's porpoises and a host of other wildlife, as well as the whales themselves. They all had a habit of flying or swimming past just as we started to dispose of the latest feast. Their sudden appearances worked on the well-known wildlife photographer's principle that, after hours of waiting patiently for something to happen, the moment you begin to do something else, like eat a sandwich, the wildlife in question jumps, or yawns, or lifts its leg, or does whatever else it was that you wanted it to do in the first place.

The Dall's porpoises were a special challenge. We knew they were nearby – sometimes, in fact, all around the boat – but we could never see them. They were almost hyperactive, there one minute, zig-zagging and darting around all over the place, and gone the next. When they rose to the surface to breathe, they moved so fast and created such a spray of water that all we saw was a wet black and white blur. I have seen many pictures of Dall's porpoises over the years – they are superficially similar to killer whales, though much smaller – but after innumerable close encounters with them in the wild I am still none the wiser.

We saw a variety of orca pods and sub-pods, including the C5s, C10s, A30s, three of the A36s, several of the A1s and four of the A12s. Most of the A5s were around during my stay as well, including A5 himself. Each pod is named after its most distinctive member and, sure enough, A5 was reasonably easy to recognise. His real name is Top Notch because, as you might guess, he has a little notch right at the top of his

The Gikumi *in the company of the most powerful predator on Earth.*

fin. Male orcas have huge dorsal fins, shaped rather like isosceles triangles, which are all slightly different in shape and often have unique scratches and scars. They make their owners instantly recognisable, often from a considerable distance. Actually, that is not strictly true - they are instantly recognisable to people who see them every day, year after year, but not to people who overdose on dozens of different fins for two weeks and then go home. Every time Bill identified a whale we had seen before, I convinced myself that I could recognise it as well. When he said 'That's A31' or 'That's A6' I wholeheartedly agreed with his diagnosis; all I needed was for him to whisper a name, or a number, and I could make a positive ID. But the problem was that if he had told me A31 was really A38 I would have believed him just the same.

Top Notch was born in 1957, so he was a couple of years older than me. He was a huge animal, weighing seven or eight tons, and so was also slightly heavier than me. He measured 25 feet or more in length. When we saw him he was with his younger half-brother, Foster, who was born in 1972 and had a smaller, slightly curved dorsal fin with no peculiar scratches or scars. Since their mother Eve died (she was found dead on a beach in 1990) the two animals have apparently spent a great deal of time together, travelling independently of the main group.

We followed Top Notch and Foster for some time as they led us to an area about a dozen miles down the coast from Telegraph Cove, called Robson Bight Ecological Reserve. This is the only orca reserve in the world. Established in 1982, it consists of 3,000 acres of sea and another 1,000 acres of land, which was added a few years later to act as a buffer zone. Whale watch boats are not allowed to enter the reserve, so we watched quietly from the sidelines.

There was another whale already in the area and, from the deck of the boat, we could actually hear the three of them talking underwater: a muffled, high-pitched whistling sound. Bill dropped a hydrophone overboard and, as we listened to their whistles, clicks and squeaks, he told us a little about our new acquaintance. It was Corky's mother, a female called Stripe. Born in 1950, Stripe was still a leading member of A5 pod. At first, she seemed to be in the reserve alone, taking time off from her duties, but then Bill pointed out another, much smaller whale, lolling in the water some distance away; it was Fife, her calf and the most recent addition to the family, born in spring 1992.

Robson Bight is famous for its 'rubbing beach', and is a regular gathering ground for many different pods. In human terms, it is like an underwater massage parlour, where the whales rub themselves on pebbles close to shore. Why they do it is something of a mystery. It is unlikely that they *need* a good rub because they do not suffer from skin parasites or barnacles, so they probably do it for pleasure. Some captive orcas seem to love the tactile stimulation of a scrubbing brush or a strong jet of water, and wild ones may enjoy the sensation of the pebbles in exactly the same way. We could not actually see what the three animals were doing underwater but, as we watched, they took it in turns to visit the beach. Top Notch and Foster lay motionless on the surface first, while Stripe swam inshore and disappeared from view. When she returned, Top Notch had a go, and then Foster, and then they each had another go, and then another.

We stayed with them for nearly half an hour and it was early evening before Bill turned the boat around and we headed back towards Telegraph Cove. There was an apricot sunset and the colours of the sky were reflected on the water and mountains all around us. The woman from Phoenix had barely uttered a word since our original encounter with the A5 pod but, for the first time that day, literally *everyone* was silent. I think we were all feeling a little overwhelmed by what we had seen.

We were still deep in our own thoughts when there was an almighty shriek from the back of the boat. I thought someone had fallen overboard but, as we all stampeded along the deck to find out what had happened, I suddenly saw Foster. He was riding in our wake – not just playing in the surf, but swimming with his nose pressed right up against the stern of the boat. Several people were already leaning over the back and almost touching him as he twisted to the left, and then to the right, and then turned completely upside-down. After several minutes, he pulled back and did an arc-shaped leap, closely followed by a complete breach; everyone gasped as he launched himself high into the air and landed back in the water with an Olympian splash. But the show was over and, by the time he resurfaced, he was already heading back towards Robson Bight.

Orcas, Bill told us, like a good sunset. It makes them do strange things and the more colourful the sky the more exuberant and full of life they seem to feel. Just like people, really.

Since 1961, a staggering 127 orcas have been captured in the wild - most of them for public display. Today, nearly 100 of those animals are dead. Yet many of their wild relatives are still alive and well and living in the same family groups that the captives were forced to leave behind.

Fifty-six of these ill-fated animals were removed from the waters of British Columbia and nearby Washington State. A5 pod suffered more than most. In 1968, six of its family members were captured and taken into captivity; they have all since died. A year later, another six were taken; four of these have also died. The only two survivors are Corky, at Sea World in San Diego, and Yaka, at Marine World near San Francisco. They have both been in captivity for nearly a quarter of a century.

Yaka spent the first 10 years of her captive life with a male called Nepo, who was also a member of A5 pod. But Nepo died, in 1980, at the very early age of 13. He was replaced by an Icelandic female called Vigga, who has been Yaka's companion ever since.

Corky was held for 16 years in a cylindrical concrete tank at a marine park near Los Angeles. Her companion was yet another member of A5 pod, a male called Orky. The two animals were moved to San Diego early in 1987, but Orky died just 18 months later; observers at the time said that Corky was deeply affected by his death. To make matters worse, during a public show soon afterwards, she was attacked by a female orca called Kandu; less than an hour later, Kandu died from massive internal bleeding. Despite thousands of hours of study, this kind of aggressive behaviour has never been observed in the wild and the attack must have been desperately upsetting for Corky. On top of all this, during her many

ORCA WATERS –
Canada

ABOVE: *Despite its fearsome reputation, the killer whale never hunts people; no-one knows why.*

ABOVE: *Killer whale country: sandwiches and lectures on the deck of the whale watch boat.*

LEFT: *Biologists have been studying some of Vancouver Island's killer whales for more than twenty years, and the animals are like old friends; this is Strider, a well-known member of A1 pod.*

RIGHT: *No matter how many times you see killer whales, they always leave your brain grappling with the improbability that anything so powerful, so beautiful and so graceful could all be rolled into one.*

BIG-WINGED NEW ENGLANDER – **USA**

RIGHT: *Humpbacks are known in the scientific world as* Megaptera novaeangliae *which, literally translated, means 'big-winged New Englander'; their knobbly white flippers are so outrageously long that they really do resemble wings.*

BELOW: *According to Herman Melville, who mentioned humpbacks in* Moby Dick, *they are 'the most gamesome and light-hearted of all the whales, making more gay foam and white water generally than any of them'.*

RIGHT: Lunchtime on Stellwagen Bank, a huge underwater restaurant for whales.

RIGHT: A humpback receiving too much love and attention.

ABOVE: *The black and white markings on the underside of a humpback's tail are so distinctive that they can be used like fingerprints, to tell one animal from another.*

RIGHT: *Mason fires a biopsy dart at a passing humpback whale, as part of an international research project to monitor the health of the population and to find out who is related to whom.*

BELOW: *New England's whales are kept under the watchful eye of teams of scientists and hordes of tourists every day throughout the summer.*

BELOW: *Some people phoned up beforehand to find out how many whales they were going to see and what they would be doing; this one is diving, though it hadn't told anyone in advance.*

RIGHT: *The Atlantic white-sided dolphin should really have been called the Atlantic multi-coloured dolphin, for obvious reasons.*

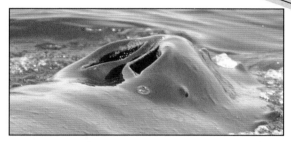

BELOW: *Looking down a humpback whale's nose; the blowholes are about the size of rabbit burrows.*

BELOW: *A humpback whale making dozens of friends for life.*

LEFT: *Breach! A humpback whale trying to turn normal, quiet, unflappable people into delirious, jabbering extroverts.*

ABOVE: *The fin whale, the second largest animal on earth, is a businesslike whale that rarely spends much time playing or people watching.*

RIGHT: *Captain Steve Sears about to embark on his 1,500th whale watching trip.*

years in captivity, she has had six unsuccessful pregnancies: one aborted foetus; a still-birth; and four live calves which, tragically, all died within a few weeks or months of birth.

Having witnessed the freedom and harmony of killer whales in the wild, the confinement of Corky, Yaka and all the other captive orcas has been haunting me ever since. While the whales they left behind are swimming in the open sea, the captives have nowhere to go in their bare and featureless tanks. They should be living in close-knit family groups, but their families have been torn apart.

Many dedicated people and organisations are battling to set them free. It could take years of negotiation, or it may never happen at all. But, in the meantime, someone has had a bright idea. Why not set up a radio link between one of the captives and its faraway family living off the coast of Vancouver Island? Corky or Yaka, imprisoned in their concrete tanks, could talk to Licka, Stripe and the rest of A5 pod – for the first time in more than 25 years.

A long-distance whale call may seem a little far-fetched, and the marine parks would probably balk at the idea, but it could be done. It would simply involve putting a radio microphone inside the concrete tank of the captive whale and then trailing a second one beside wild members of its home pod in Johnstone Strait.

The animals would certainly speak the same language: even after all these years, both Corky and Yaka still retain the full repertoire of A5's various calls. The phrases they use may be a little old fashioned and quaint, and they have learned some Icelandic in the meantime, but there is little doubt that they would be understood.

The only question that remains is this: if Corky or Yaka were given a chance to make that call, what would they say?

Big-winged New Englander

HUMPBACK WHALES OFF AMERICA'S EAST COAST

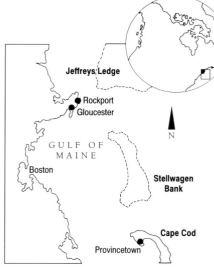

THERE IS A LARGE underwater plateau in the middle of Massachusetts Bay, called Stellwagen Bank. It is shaped rather like a wrinkled pear and points vaguely north-west. Although just 25 miles from the skyscrapers of Boston, it is well hidden beneath the ocean waves and therefore impossible to find on a map.

Stellwagen is a kind of underwater restaurant for whales. Every summer, huge numbers of humpback, fin and minke whales gather in its shallow waters to gorge themselves on vast shoals of fish. Endangered northern right whales, Atlantic white-sided dolphins and a number of other species also dine in the area from time to time.

Built during the last Ice Age, the restaurant consists of a huge pile of sand and gravel, about 18 miles long and up to six miles wide, resting on the seabed. The top of the pile is roughly 100 feet below the surface and is more or less flat, like a table top; the sides are steep and drop towards the surrounding seabed, 200 feet deeper, like a long table cloth. As the tidal currents surge in and out of Massachusetts Bay, they hit the sides of Stellwagen and force cold water from near the seabed up towards the surface. This carries nutrients to the sun-soaked layers above the plateau, and forms the basis of an amazingly productive food chain.

For the visiting whales, the most important link in the chain is a small, worm-like fish called a sand eel, or sand lance. This is a strange creature, about the length and shape of a fountain pen, with a long, floppy dorsal fin along its back. A huge whale, of course, would hardly notice if it swallowed something so small. But sand eels are gregarious by nature and like plenty of company, so all the whale has to do for a good hearty meal is to swim through a sand eel get-together, with its mouth wide open, and it can swallow thousands of the hapless animals in a single gulp.

For the visiting whale watchers, the most important link in the food chain is the humpback. If anyone planned to design the perfect whale for whale watching they would probably be wasting their time, because it has already been done. The humpback is: a) easy to find; b) outrageously inquisitive (if whales had curtains it would spend hours every day peeping through the gap in the middle); and c) capable of performing some of the most spectacular acrobatic displays on Earth. Some humpback whales have not read the appropriate field guides and are: a) extremely difficult to find; b) outrageously indifferent to whale watchers; and c) couch potatoes. But there are exceptions to every rule. Herman Melville, who mentioned them in *Moby Dick*, knew what he was talking about when he described them as 'the most gamesome and lighthearted of all the whales, making more gay foam and white water generally than any of them'.

The humpbacks' underwater restaurant is within easy reach of almost every coastal town in Massachusetts, New Hampshire and Maine and, in recent years, has become the focus of one of the most competitive whale watching markets in the world. It attracts nearly 1.5 million whale watchers every year. The whales are kept under the watchful eye of teams of scientists and hordes of tourists every day from the end of April to mid-October, and there are literally dozens of small charter companies, research groups, wildlife organisations and huge commercial operators running tours to see them.

I spent several weeks in a small Massachusetts town called Gloucester, on the rocky coast of Cape Ann. Established in the early 1620s, by settlers who named it after their home town in England, Gloucester is America's oldest seaport. It lies just 12 miles north-west of Stellwagen Bank and boasts five commercial whale watching companies with a total of 16 boats. I joined more than 1,000 whale watchers and dozens of humpbacks on Stellwagen Bank every day.

A humpback whale flipper-slapping on Stellwagen Bank.

I was standing on the upper deck of the *Miss Cape Ann III*, watching a long line of people clamber down a steep ramp that led from the jetty to the catamaran.

The first on board was an unshaven man in his late twenties, dressed in army fatigues; he had a rifle grip with a huge camera lens thrown over his shoulder, like a bazooka, and a tattoo of a spider on his left cheek. Behind him was a young couple with three crying toddlers in an enormous triple pushchair; their exasperated father was trying to lift them over the railings and onto the boat while their mother screeched instructions from behind. Then there was an elderly couple with gnarled walking sticks and a pair of the largest binoculars on the East Coast. They were followed by two men carrying a huge ice box about half the size of a coffin; as their beer bellies wobbled on the lid, and beads of sweat rolled down from under their baseball caps, they wrestled it off the crowded ramp and onto the steps of the boat.

I felt like Noah keeping a discreet eye on the loading of the Ark.

Everyone headed immediately for the upper deck. It was something that happened on every trip. While the lower deck was like an open-air cinema about to show an educational film on tapeworms, people fought over the seats on the upper deck as if they were embroiled in a life or death game of musical chairs. There they sat, afraid to move in case another whale watcher tried to steal their place, in a battle of nerves that lasted for the hour-long ride out to Stellwagen Bank. The irony was that, while the upper deck was important-looking and irrefutably high, it was also a long way from the sea and a million miles from all the action. So, when the first whales came alongside, there was always a great deal of pushing and shoving as everyone scrambled down to the lower deck for a better view, leaving a jumble of handbags, camera cases, wallets and chairs scattered in their wake.

We were travelling with *Captain Bill's Whale Watch*. Having found whales on all but a handful of occasions since its first commercial trip in 1979, *Captain Bill's* had earned itself one of the best sightings records in town. The *Miss Cape Ann III* was the pride and joy of the fleet. A custom-built catamaran, with a painting of a female humpback and her calf adorning the bridge, she was about 70 feet long and licensed to carry no fewer than 147 passengers and five crew. With skipper Steve Sears at the helm, we cruised past a row of wooden houses lining the coast, picked our way through a maze of floats marking lobster pots in the harbour entrance and headed out to sea.

Steve, who was soon to embark on his 1,500th whale watch, spent most of the time on the radio. Information about recent sightings, from local fishermen and other whale watchers, crackled across the airwaves as he jotted down the coordinates on a scrap of paper. But the radio talk was about more than locating whales. It was about specific whales - individuals that every skipper and all the local biologists knew by name.

Skippers and whale biologists are able to recognise one another by their faces; some have red noses, others have long, straggly beards, a few are completely bald and several wear make-up. With a little practice, it is quite easy to tell them apart. Unfortunately, humpback whales do not have such distinctive faces; but, instead, they are recognisable by the unique black and white markings on the underside of their tails. These range from jet black to pure white and include an endless number of variations in between. No two humpbacks have identical markings and, with experience, it is possible to tell one animal from another simply by peering underneath as they lift their tails high into the air in preparation for a deep dive.

Biologists have been identifying individual animals as part of their research for many years. Jane Goodall used facial patterns to recognise all the chimpanzees in her classic study in Gombe National Park, Tanzania; she found that each member of the group had a distinctive haircut, as well as a recognisable mouth and nose, and unique eyes and ears. More recent studies have used striping patterns in zebras, the arrangement of whiskers in lions and even the shapes, nicks and scars of elephants' ears to tell one animal from another. In fact, many field biologists have become so proficient at recognising individuals that 'their' animals might as well be carrying passports.

Whale researchers have already catalogued nearly 1,000 humpbacks in the area stretching from Long Island in the south, through Massachusetts Bay and all the way to Nova Scotia in the north. More are being added to the list all the time.

They give the animals names, which are all mnemonic. Cat's Paw, for example, has a jet black tail interrupted only by a white paw print on the lefthand side; Fracture also has a black tail, but with a distinctive white line down the middle; and Seal's tail – as you might imagine – has an image of a seal on the underside. Another whale, called Silver, earned her name from the one-legged pirate Long John Silver, after she survived a collision with a boat that sliced off one of her flukes. I did not see Silver (she had washed ashore on 30 May 1991, entangled in marine debris) but she was much talked about on Stellwagen Bank; she had been a regular visitor for more than a decade and became the first known grandmother when her 1980 calf, called Beltane, returned in 1985 with a calf of her own.

There are only two rules in the humpback whale naming game. The first is that human names, like Bert or Beryl, are not allowed because they are considered too anthropomorphic. The second is that names which assume the sex of the animal, like Dr. Spock or Lady Chatterley, are also not allowed because it is usually impossible to tell the difference (unless the whale turns up with a calf, in which case it is a female). Otherwise, anything goes.

But there is more to naming humpbacks than pure scientific logic. Once a year there is a party for whale biologists from up and down the East Coast. They arrive clutching bundles of photographs, laptop computers and bottles of champagne, talk incessantly about humpbacks and reminisce about good times with Cat's Paw, Fracture and friends. But the main purpose of their annual gathering is to agree on a name for each new whale identified during the previous season. One by one, the animals are considered and discussed. To insiders it is a complicated and stringent process, developed with painstaking care and attention to detail over a period of many years. But to outsiders what basically happens is that the biologist who shouts the loudest, or bickers the longest, chooses the new name. Then everyone toasts the whale with a glass of champagne.

This works pretty well for the first 20 or 30 whales. After that, imaginations run a little wild. The best way to tell how late in the party a whale was christened is by the length of time it takes for the biologists to explain their logic in selecting its name. Pegasus was probably named around midnight (I never could work out the indecipherable pattern of scratches and scars that are supposed to resemble the heavenly constellation of the same name); and I expect Dash-dot was named at around two o'clock in the morning, judging by the two dashes and a dot that are completely hidden among a jumble of other dashes and dots, long lines, semi-circles, smudges, scratches and scars. Other early-hours-of-the-morning whales include Helios, Tear, Latitude, Firefly, Pole, Coral, Bittern, Zepellin, Nine, Rocker, Nile, Molson, Guinness, Bamboo and, indeed, to my untrained eye, most of the other humpbacks around Stellwagen Bank.

Young whales pose a particular problem, not least because their tail patterns change as they grow older. One female, called Talon, began life with a tail that was one-third white; but within a year it had turned completely black. This is the kind of problem that is welcomed by the biologists, who have to toast the whale again the following year.

Purists might argue that the use of names encourages biologists to become too attached to their subjects. But imagine finding a whale out on Stellwagen Bank and then trying to remember, with a complete absence of visual clues, whether it is number 673 or 464. Worse still, try racking your brain to distinguish between WP14ZF and XY55PT. It would be impossible.

At the same time, it is impossible *not* to become attached. Anyone who has had a close encounter with a humpback, just once, finds it hard to remain emotionally stable for several weeks, or even months, afterwards. So biologists who see them every day would have to be made of stone not to be affected. It simply does not make any difference whether the whale is called Number 673, Special Code WP14ZF or simply Cat's Paw. Many of the biologists I met working on Stellwagen Bank admitted to being utterly preoccupied with the whales. They think about them from the moment they get up in the morning until the time they go to bed at night; they talk about them at breakfast, lunch and supper; and they even dream about them in their sleep.

I became emotionally attached to a whale called Salt. The grand old lady of New England humpbacks, Salt is the most consistently sighted whale on Stellwagen Bank. She has been returning to the area every summer since her first appearance on 1 May 1976 and, after nearly 20 years, may well be the most researched whale in the world. Named after a distinctive white patch and a sprinkling of white spots on her dorsal fin (in the days before anyone had thought of using the markings underneath the tail) Salt was the first individual humpback to be officially identified and given a name. The white patch looks rather like dried sea salt and is so distinctive that even I could recognise her at sea.

In fact, Salt was the first humpback I met during the trip. As we were leaving the harbour, a fisherman radioed Steve to say that she was loafing around the northern tip of the Bank. It was a clear day, with calm seas, and less than an hour after receiving the message her wispy blows were clearly visible just below the horizon, though it was several minutes before we could see Salt herself.

The *Miss Cape Ann III* slowed to an idle pace and Steve cut the engines. As we drifted, Salt turned slightly and began to swim straight towards us. After the mass exodus from the upper deck, a few people whistled and cheered, and then there was a stunned silence as the great whale came to within a few yards of the boat. Rolling onto her side, she kept one eye above the surface of the water and had a long, thoughtful look at the row of enthralled faces staring back. Then she dipped out of sight and swam right underneath the boat. I leant inside the bridge, behind Steve, just in time to see her blurry shape pass across the sonar screen: she was no more than 30 feet below the hull.

One hundred and forty seven whale watchers scampered across the deck and watched as she resurfaced on the other side. She hesitated, as if wondering what to do next, then gently rolled onto her back and, in one sweeping movement, lifted her enormous knobbly white flippers high into the air.

Humpbacks are known in the scientific world as *Megaptera novaeangliae* which, literally translated, means 'big-winged New Englander'. Their flippers are so outrageously long (Salt's measured about 15 feet) that they really do resemble wings; viewed from the air, a group of swimming humpbacks looks surpisingly like a formation of Jumbo jets. (Incidentally, 'New Englander' is also appropriate because, although humpbacks are found in many parts of the world, they were first scientifically described from an animal that stranded on the New England coast during the 18th century).

Salt spent nearly ten minutes lolling upside-down, with her great wings pointing skyward, before she slapped one of them onto the surface of the water and then rolled around onto her front. The show, apparently, was over. She swam forward slightly, dipped her head below the surface, lifted her tail – which measures an incredible 12 feet from tip to tip – and disappeared from view.

On the trail of the humpback whale.

For several years, no-one knew whether Salt was male or female. It was not until 1980, when she turned up with a calf by her side (later named Crystal, because it was a little piece of Salt) that she disclosed her well-kept secret. She has had many calves since – Thalassa, Halos, Bittern and Salsa – and, when Thalassa had a calf of her own in 1992, she became a grandmother for the first time. When I saw her, she appeared to be pregnant yet again.

Salt will go down in history as the whale that confirmed a link between the humpback feeding grounds on Stellwagen Bank and their breeding grounds 1,500 miles away in the Caribbean. Biologists had long suspected that they migrated between the two places twice every year, but there was no firm evidence until Salt was positively identified, in 1978, off the coast of the Dominican Republic. More recent evidence has shown that the warm waters of the Caribbean, over shallow banks off the coasts of the Dominican Republic, Puerto Rico and the Virgin Islands, are the most important winter breeding grounds for humpbacks from all over the North Atlantic. Every year, the whales spend three or four months there before returning to their feeding grounds in the spring.

One of the great pleasures for whale biologists working on Stellwagen Bank is being able to watch old friends arrive back safely after their long winter absence.

Biologist Mason Weinrich has been there to greet them for nearly 15 years. Director of the Cetacean Research Unit (CRU), based in Gloucester, Mason is the kind of person who reads books about whale droppings on his days off. He has been studying Stellwagen's humpbacks since the late 1970s and is on first-name terms with most of the animals on his 'patch'.

CRU is a non-profit organisation set up to study and conserve the endangered whales of New England. Its work relies on an ingenious, and usually happy, marriage between research and whale watching. As part of a long-standing arrangement with *Captain Bill's*, Mason or a member of his team accompanies every whale watching trip, providing a non-stop commentary that begins with an introductory talk on the dockside and ends with a summary of the sightings of the day. Over the years, they have made presentations to more than a quarter of a million people. In return, the whale watching boats provide an excellent platform for research, enabling CRU biologists to gather extensive field notes for their own work. In fact, most of our knowledge about the whales of Massachusetts Bay (which are among the most extensively studied whales in the world) has been learned from observations made during commercial trips such as these.

It is hard work studying whales and pandering to whale watchers at the same time. The CRU biologists had to hold a microphone in one hand, and repeat the same basic information twice every day, seven days a week (while making it sound as if they were saying it for the very first time) and they had to hold a camera in the other hand to take identification photographs of every whale's tail. In between, they had to answer an endless stream of questions from passengers, dictate notes to their research assistant, liaise with the skipper and, for a couple of weeks at least, trip over all my camera equipment.

Photography is a very important part of their work, providing a permanent record of every humpback whale observed. All the pictures go to a central library of identification photographs, housed at the College of the Atlantic in Bar Harbour, Maine. A large network of research organisations and biologists from all over the North Atlantic contributes to this fantastic store of information. In return, all the contributors receive details on the movements and activities of 'their' whales, whenever they have been spotted in someone else's study area. It is a real team effort. Similar libraries also exist for humpbacks living in the North Pacific and the Southern Ocean.

In many ways, the library is like an enormous jigsaw puzzle. It is packed with snippets of information – field notes as well as photographs – which, carefully pieced together, can provide an overall picture of individual whales, family groups and even entire populations. The records help biologists to follow their daily and seasonal movements, to measure the rate of growth of a calf from one year to the next, to find out if certain animals have unusual behaviour patterns and to gain an insight into many other aspects of their lives.

It is also a critical source of information for one of the most ambitious studies of whales ever undertaken. Dubbed YONAH – Years of the North Atlantic Humpback – this exciting study began in 1992 and involves biologists in the West Indies, the United States, Canada, Greenland, Iceland and Norway. The idea is to examine the health of all the main humpback populations in the North Atlantic.

Photographs and field observations are an important part of YONAH, but the biologists also have to take small samples of whale skin. This is for a new area of research called 'DNA fingerprinting' or 'genetic fingerprinting', which is already being used in human paternity and criminal cases. The aim is to learn more about whale family trees by working out who is related to whom.

Mason invited me to join him on a special research trip to obtain some skin samples for the study and we arranged to meet at a jetty, on the outskirts of Gloucester, at 4.30 the following morning.

The least sensitive part of a humpback whale.

One of the problems with being a biologist is the constant lack of sleep. You are always having to get up early in the morning and if you dare to mention the possibility of a lie-in to other biologists they treat you with contempt for the rest of the day. After a while, you just learn to sleep fast and keep quiet.

It was still dark when I rolled up, lifeless and uncommunicative, at the appointed hour. Mason had already stowed away the equipment and was busily untying the research boat from the jetty. Called *Silver I*, in memory of Silver the one-fluked whale, the boat was about 20 feet long and had a large outboard motor and a rather worn and well-used look about it. All the pleasure crafts that were tied alongside looked much the same. But *Silver I* was special. Nearly 20 years old, it had been used regularly by CRU since 1984, clocking up thousands of hours of research time.

We arrived on the farther reaches of Stellwagen Bank as the first light of dawn began to show above the horizon. Mason has a reputation for conjuring whales out of nowhere and, before I had even started looking, he spotted a group of five humpbacks heading in our direction. He cut the engine and, as we sat there in the brightening orange glow of the early morning sun, more than 20 miles from shore, the whales came closer and closer until they were almost within touching distance. They were at least twice the length and many times the weight of our tiny boat and, when one accidentally thumped the side with its tail, for a brief moment I felt really small and vulnerable.

I began to worry about the unpleasant surprise we had in store for them. They were so trusting, and I felt guilty.

A skin sample is obtained by firing a small metal arrow, called a biopsy dart, into the whale's skin. Mason was using a crossbow to fire the dart and, while I steadied the boat at a distance of about 25 feet, he took aim at the first whale. It was a large target, especially at such close range. But whales are very sentient animals and Mason had to be careful to hit a large cushion of fat just below the dorsal fin, where the skin is believed to be the least sensitive. As soon as the whale lifted its tail for a deep dive, he fired. There was a slight thud, the huge animal flinched very slightly and the dart bounced backwards and into the water. With Mason back at the controls, manoeuvring the boat into position, I leaned over the side and grabbed the dart as it floated on the surface.

We crouched next to a row of test tubes and solutions laid out on the deck, as Mason carefully removed the tiny sample of skin with a pair of tweezers. There was a small plug of blubber in there as well, and this he kept for later analysis to measure pollution levels in the whale's body. Once the two samples had been labelled and filed away, he sterilised the dart and we were ready for our next 'patient'.

During the morning, we managed to dart all five whales. Three of them flinched slightly, or flicked their tails, but when they resurfaced several minutes later they appeared to be none the worse for their experience. The other two showed no reaction at all. None of them seemed to associate the darts with the boat and they continued to be as trusting and friendly as before.

DNA fingerprinting is a complex process that requires detailed analysis of the skin samples in a laboratory. The DNA itself is a kind of instruction manual for the design and assembly of the body's proteins. Every cell in an animal's body contains an exact replica of this manual and almost all the 'pages' go to making it what it is – a person, a cat, a whale, and so on. But the small number of pages that are left help to distinguish one individual from another. Just as one person's fingerprints are different from everyone else's, no two animals have exactly the same DNA. The differences are incredibly small but, with chemical analysis, it is possible to find them. Then it is a matter of clever detective work to find out exactly what those differences mean.

The key to DNA fingerprinting is that half the 'fingerprint' originates from the mother and the other half from the father. This means that two whale calves with both the same mother and the same father would have extremely similar (though not identical) 'fingerprints'; if the calves had the same mother but a different father, only half would be similar; distantly-related animals would have some, but much less, similarity; and so on.

The aim of the study is to answer a number of important questions. Do different calves with the same mother have the same father? Are individuals that spend a great deal of time together closely related? Do the fathers have any direct contact with their calves? And many more.

Some of these questions are being answered already. For example, it has been confirmed that two calves, born in 1981 and 1988, both have the same mother but they have different fathers. This would suggest that male and female humpbacks do not mate for life. Many more skin samples will have to be taken before a theory such as this can be tested properly, but the potential for DNA fingerprinting in humpback whale research is tantalizing. Most of all, it could provide information about the lives and habits of these endangered animals that may prove invaluable to future conservation efforts.

The next day was a baking hot Sunday. By mid-morning Stellwagen Bank was so crowded there was barely enough room for the catamaran to move. It was like whale watching in a sardine tin. The northern tip of the Bank reminded me of a children's boating lake, with brightly-coloured speedboats, motor cruisers, yachts and an infinite number of other vessels spread out across the water in every direction. I tried counting them - but gave up after reaching four hundred.

People were fishing, sailing and whale watching. There were many more whale watchers than whales and, everywhere we went, the catamaran was followed by a flotilla of private boats whose owners seemed incapable of finding the animals on their own. A couple of times Steve tried to shake them off by cutting the engines and glaring. But every time a whale came up for air it was quickly surrounded by our hangers-on, like a pride of Kenyan lions being set upon by a gang of black-and-white striped mini-buses.

There have been many efforts to regulate whale watching on Stellwagen Bank, before it escalates out of control. The aim has always been to provide an acceptable measure of protection for the animals while still allowing people to observe them. It is already illegal to harass a whale (anyone found guilty is liable to a fine of up to $20,000 and two years in prison) though enforcement of the law is rather hit and miss. Since the problem seems to be caused as much by a general lack of awareness as by people who are consciously harming the animals, there are also simple guidelines explaining how day-trippers can keep disturbance to a minimum. A leaflet – appropriately entitled 'Too Close for Comfort!' – is distributed to boaters every weekend during the summer; it explains how to handle a boat around whales and has plenty of gruesome pictures to spell out the dangers of getting too close.

A six-year old whale, called Latitude, seemed especially unhappy with all the attention. Latitude was popular with the commercial whale watch operators and Steve considered her to be an honorary member of the 'team'. But the crowds were proving too much, even for an extrovert like her, and she was diving for much longer than usual and changing direction underwater to avoid the onslaught.

Watching Latitude, and some of the other whales we encountered during the day, it became clear that most of them were troubled by irresponsible boat handling rather than by the size of the boats themselves. My first impression of the *Miss Cape Ann III* had been of a huge monster that would frighten the living daylights out of every sensible whale the moment it loomed over the horizon. But with Steve at the helm, the 'monster' could have been another whale for all the disturbance it caused. Like most of the other professional skippers, Steve knew how to behave around humpbacks. He manoeuvred his enormous vessel impeccably, taking great care to give the animals plenty of space, never to approach them head-on and to avoid excessive speed or sudden changes in direction; then, after 10 or 15 minutes, he left them in peace. He took his responsibilities seriously, and even kept a watchful eye on his colleagues to ensure that they did the same.

Most of the day-trippers probably meant the whales no harm. They were either careless or simply had no idea what they were doing. But some terrible injuries have been reported after collisions with private boats. I saw one particularly irresponsible man, in a flashy yellow speedboat, who should have been thrown overboard years ago. Showing off to his passengers, he was trying to motor alongside a female humpback and her young calf. The two animals were clearly distressed, swimming fast and taking short, snatched breaths, but wherever they went he was just a few yards behind. Suddenly, they surfaced right in front of his boat and he was so busy preening his ego that he failed to notice. Instead of slowing down he ran straight over their backs.

Somehow, the two whales escaped unscathed. But it was more by luck than judgement.

His brainless stunt was performed in full view of the catamaran, with nearly 150 horrified passengers watching his every move. It was the only time I ever saw Steve lose his temper. He gave the man a stiff lecture about respecting the whales instead of harassing them and, predictably, received a barrage of abuse in reply.

No two whale watching trips were alike. In the morning, we could find a single humpback and nothing else; in the afternoon, there could be dozens of them stretched almost flipper-to-flipper across the width of the Bank. They could be lolling around on the surface like sunbathers floating on blow-up sunbeds, or they could be in a frenzy of activity from the moment we arrived to the frustrating moment we had to leave.

Other species appeared from time to time as well. One morning we saw humpbacks, minke whales, fin whales and Atlantic white-sided dolphins – all in the space of just two hours.

Minke whales are the smallest of the great whales found regularly on Stellwagen Bank. Of course, they are by no means small by everyday standards, but even a 25-foot, eight-ton whale is dwarfed by some of its larger relatives. Most of the minkes I saw were little more than grey-brown blobs in the distance, although sometimes there was a fleeting glimpse of a curved dorsal fin thrown in for good measure. The best sighting was when a minke crossed in front of the bow and surfaced immediately below a crowd of people squashed into one of the catamaran's pulpits; it was just possible to make out the white band across one of its flippers – a feature common to all minkes in the northern hemisphere, making them look as if they are wearing white arm bands.

Two minke whales lying end-to-end would still be shorter than a fin whale, which is the second largest animal on earth (after the blue whale). You would have to add a couple of people lying end-to-end as well to make up the difference. The fin is a businesslike whale that rarely wastes much time playing or people watching. It treats boats as an estate agent would treat a client trying to speed up the sale of his house – with complete indifference. The fin whales we saw confidently swam alongside the boat but always seemed to have urgent business to attend to and hurried along instead of stopping to pass the time of day. (It is probably just a coincidence, but all the rushing around seems to do them a lot of good – because they are much slimmer than humpback whales).

Two humpbacks swimming flipper-to-flipper under the watchful eye of hordes of tourists.

The other interesting thing about fin whales is their colour. Whoever painted their right jaw white forgot to do the same on the other side, which is dark grey or black. This makes them one of the few whales, which are asymmetrical.

Studying fin whales is even more difficult than studying humpbacks and, consequently, our knowledge about them is very patchy. For a start, we do not even know where they go in the winter. They are easy to find (look for a tall, thin blow about as high as the guttering on a two-storey house) but they take no more than two or three breaths between dives and then change direction underwater, making them almost impossible to approach closely. Someone could make a lot of money by taking bets from unsuspecting whale watchers prepared to guess where a fin whale is going to surface next.

It is also very difficult to tell one fin whale from another. Unlike humpbacks, their tails do not have distinctive 'fingerprints' (and, come to think of it, even if they did, no-one would be able to see the markings because they never lift their tails out of the water). But recent research has revealed a possible alternative. There is a white streak, known as a chevron, that runs from just behind the blowhole, along the upper back and then down each side of every fin whale. The extent and shape of the chevron varies slightly from one animal to the next and, although the differences are very subtle, it is just possible to distinguish between individuals by scrutinising photographs of them back on shore. It is painstaking work, but the results could be quite revealing.

We found white-sided dolphins about once every two or three days. Actually, to say that we found them is not strictly true. They found us. Small groups of 40 or 50 dolphins would appear from nowhere, racing across the sea to perform spectacular acrobatic displays next to the boat and to ride in our bow waves. If there were any fin whales around they would ride in their bow waves too; the whales pretended not to notice, although they did look a little agitated when the hyperactive dolphins began to jump over their heads. I once saw three of them leap in a perfectly coordinated group right over the head of a fin whale, and then jump back again.

The Atlantic white-sided dolphin's name does not do it justice. For some reason, it was named after a rather dull creamy-white stripe down its side, but in fact it is a striking creature coloured with a stunning mixture of black, white, grey and yellow. It should really have been called the Atlantic multi-coloured dolphin. Perhaps there are parties for biologists to toast the names of new *species* with glasses of champagne?

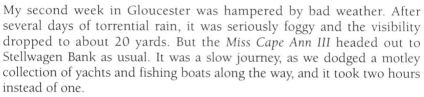

My second week in Gloucester was hampered by bad weather. After several days of torrential rain, it was seriously foggy and the visibility dropped to about 20 yards. But the *Miss Cape Ann III* headed out to Stellwagen Bank as usual. It was a slow journey, as we dodged a motley collection of yachts and fishing boats along the way, and it took two hours instead of one.

Steve cut the engines and, as we drifted, Mason picked up the microphone and tried to sound positive and comforting. He confirmed that there was little chance of seeing a whale, unless one happened to surface right next to the boat, but asked us to *listen* for their blows instead. Then he called for silence and promptly disappeared behind a thick wall of fog.

There were despondent looks all round before everyone settled down for the inevitable long wait. Nothing much happened for half an hour or more: the silence was broken every two minutes by the catamaran's foghorn blasting its warning to an unseen world; in between, there was the muffled sound of children being scolded by their parents; also, a man suddenly shouted 'Over there!' at a passing wave, and looked around sheepishly to see if anyone had noticed his mistake (they had).

But most people were fast asleep or dozing when we heard the first unmistakable sound of a blow. It was so loud it could almost have come from underneath the boat.

Everyone was awake and staring into the fog by the time the second blow came and, with a little deft manoeuvring by Steve, we were suddenly alongside an enormous 'flukeprint' in the water. Made by the swish of a tail close to the surface, a flukeprint is the nearest a whale can get to a footprint. This particular one was 10 or 12 feet across and consisted of a circle of smooth water rather like a transparent oil slick.

It was the first in a long line of flukeprints heading into the fog. Steve was slowly working his way along the 'path' when there was a third blow, closely followed by a fourth, and two dark shapes slipped into view. I had noticed many times before that Steve seemed to have a special rapport with the whales – it was almost as if they felt obliged to surface close to the *Miss Cape Ann III* – and the two animals welcomed us by circling the boat once and then checking underneath the hull.

Mason recognised them almost immediately as a couple of old friends called Firefly and Bittern. (Mason also has a special rapport with the whales and is well-known for being able to identify them long before other people have even reached for their binoculars. On one memorable occasion, frequently talked about on Stellwagen Bank, he spotted a tail hundreds of yards from the boat and instantly recognised it as belonging to a whale called Amber; astonishingly, he and Amber had never met before – but Mason knew the black and white markings from a photograph he had seen at the annual whale-naming party the year before).

We stayed with Firefly and Bittern (or they stayed with us – it was hard to tell) for almost an hour. They were feeding for a while, their long, expandable throat grooves working like concertinas to take in massive quantities of fish and water. Once or twice their heads appeared above the surface, with water gushing from their bulging mouths, but they soon relaxed and settled down next to the boat.

As I photographed Firefly (by then lying upside-down with one flipper raised high in the air) there was a shriek from the bow. Two women in their late thirties, with matching outfits and jangling beads, were hopping and skipping around the deck. I had noticed them before and, while they seemed reasonably normal at first, they had been acting increasingly strangely ever since our first encounter with the whales. When they had finished their dance they moved to opposite sides of the boat. One sat cross-legged on the deck and murmured a wild, half-sung, half-yodelled mantra, while the other leant over the railings and whirled a four-foot piece of hosepipe around in circles. I was bursting to ask them two questions: 'What were they doing?' and, 'What the heck were they doing?'. When I finally plucked up enough courage to approach them, they talked about mystical experiences, golden energy fields, cerebral navigation, elevating vibrational levels and filling the vortex of life. I have no idea what it all meant.

After a while, Firefly and Bittern both disappeared underwater. Everyone moved away from the railings and started to rewind their films or queue up for cups of coffee. Even the two jangly women calmed down and prepared themselves for a few moments of meditation. I was busily wiping part of a peanut-butter sandwich from my T-shirt when, without warning, the man standing next to me spat out a mouthful of coffee and yelled hysterically. I thought I had accidently brushed some peanut butter onto *his* T-shirt, but turned in time to see Bittern flying through the air no more than 50 yards from the boat. The huge whale arched its back, twisted slightly and then fell into the water with a colossal splash. It seemed to move in slow motion. Its huge flippers looked like wings and the tip of its throat was somehow shaped like a bird's beak — I still have a lasting mental image of a giant, overfed parrot.

No-one knows why whales breach, though there are many different theories. It may be a form of signalling, because the noise of the splash can be heard for miles underwater; it could be a way of dislodging parasites, such as whale lice or barnacles; it might be a form of greeting or a way of saying 'goodbye'; or just possibly, it may be something the whales do purely for fun. Youngsters tend to do it more often than older animals, and rough seas seem to get them going more than calm seas. Many humpbacks find it infectious: when one animal breaches others often join in, like people who are unable to keep a straight face while someone near them is laughing. And they sometimes never seem to want to stop: one individual was seen breaching 130 times in 75 minutes.

As the water calmed down we waited, this time with cameras at the ready, for another breach. But it never came.

It was several minutes before Firefly and Bittern reappeared. They surfaced just a few yards away from an elderly woman who was sitting alone in a quiet corner of the deck. The woman watched intently as they put on another extraordinary show, this time one that seemed almost choreographed. Firefly blew a tall column of water vapour high into the air, and Bittern blew another a split second later. Firefly dived beneath the surface, flukes pointing skyward, and Bittern dived a split second later.

The woman showed no emotion and never said a word. But every time the whales took a joint curtain call, and disappeared from view, she clapped politely. Later in the morning, she confided that it had been the most exciting hour of her life.

POSTSCRIPT

STELLWAGEN BANK faces many serious threats. There is a dump site for hazardous wastes just four miles away; there are plans to pump 500 million gallons of Boston's sewage, every day, into waters that circulate around the southern end of the Bank; commercial and private boat traffic is increasing in the area at an alarming rate; and, in recent years, there have been proposals for a commercial harvest of sand eels, to build an artificial island resort, to establish a variety of aquaculture operations and for underwater sand and gravel mining. So it was fantastic news to hear that, since my visit, Stellwagen Bank has been declared a National Marine Sanctuary. This followed years of campaigning by CRU and other research and conservation organisations for this important area to be given special protection. Its new status does not solve all these environmental problems in one go, but it does at last provide the necessary framework for its protection - and some funds to put this into action.

Minke Patrol

STUDYING MINKE WHALES IN SCOTLAND

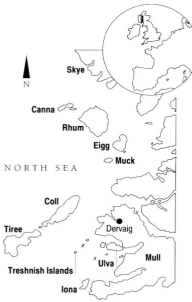

IMAGINE TWO LIVES. One is spent surrounded by people and pressures, trapped in endless queues of traffic, crushed into busy rush-hour trains, and dreaming of a better life far from the madding crowd. The other is spent on a beautiful mountainous island, surrounded by moorland, glens, lochs, forests and rocky shores, waking up to the sounds of the sea and sharing the peace and tranquility with no-one but family and friends.

Richard Fairbairns did what we have all dreamed of doing when, in the late 1970s, he abandoned the rat-race and moved to a beautiful mountainous island. The island was Mull, off the rugged west coast of Scotland, and his new neighbours were eagles, otters, seals and seabirds. He bought a boat - a 'retired gin palace' – and embarked on a new career taking people on private fishing trips and to see the abundant local wildlife.

It was hard work but, for ten years, Richard was happy developing his new business. Then he had an experience that was to change his life all over again. This time there was no planning and no conscious search for a new challenge. It just happened. He was on a fishing charter, drifting quietly in calm seas near the Isle of Coll, when a whale came over to inspect his boat. It swam around in circles, lolled in the water in front of the bow, rolled upside-down to inspect the hull and spent more than half an hour weaving carefully in and out of the fishing lines. It even popped its head out of the water, as if looking to see who was on board. Even before the animal had dived for the last time, Richard was a changed man.

He had never seen a whale before and knew nothing about them, but he was determined to find out more and spent the next few weeks buried in all the whale books he could find. Finally, he managed to identify his new acquaintance as a minke whale – one of more than 20 different whales and dolphins that can be found in the waters around Britain.

Minke whales are small compared to some of their giant-sized relatives, though they still grow to more than 25 feet in length and weigh around eight tons. They can be elusive animals and are normally so untheatrical that many whale researchers seem to find them rather boring. Consequently, few people have attempted to study them in the wild and, although fairly common in many parts of the world, minkes are remarkably poorly known. This was a revelation to Richard. How could such a sensational animal be poorly known? And to think that it was living right on his own doorstep. He could not believe his luck.

With minkes constantly on the mind, he began to see them on a regular basis and gradually built up a file of his sightings. But he needed funds to organise a proper study and, being a non-scientist, had little hope of negotiating a research grant. The solution to his problem came from North America, where whale watching vessels frequently provide a platform for research and, in some cases, even help to pay for the work. It was the perfect formula, although Richard decided to take it a stage further. He wanted to get everyone involved with the research itself – to give the whale watching a purpose and, at the same time, to benefit the project by harnessing the diverse skills of people who have never been involved with whales before.

He took the plunge in August 1989, when he gave up the fishing charters and began to concentrate on whales full-time. Now he has some funding from the International Fund for Animal Welfare, thousands of minke whale sightings under his belt and a reputation as something of an expert. But he has never forgotten the first close encounter that changed his life.

It felt as if I were back at school. But this time I was not being taught under duress and was actually enjoying myself. I had seven classmates, ranging in age from a young woman in her early twenties to a couple in their mid-seventies, and we were all on our best behaviour. No-one threw rubbers or heckled the teacher, though perhaps this was because there were no fewer than four teachers to keep us in check.

It was our first evening on Mull and we were sitting around a table in the 'Lodge' – the nerve centre of the minke project – near a little village called Dervaig. Barely a stone's throw from the sea, the Lodge was in a fabulous position on the rugged northern coast of the island.

We were not really attending a lesson so much as a crash course in minke whale research. Richard stressed that it was a working holiday – the success or failure of the project depended largely on us or, at least, on people like us. If we were to be of any help at all during the week, we did have to know a little bit about what was happening. But this did not sound like the kind of work we had all left behind for a well-earned break and, as Richard showed us pictures of minke whales, explained the procedure on the boat and then introduced the other members of the team, there was a growing sense of excitement in the classroom.

The man in charge of the research was Vassili Papastavrou, a biologist who had previously studied whales in the Indian Ocean, the Galapagos Islands, the Azores and several other places around the world; the west coast of Scotland was not his most exotic posting. Helping Vassili, as the research assistant, was a young New Zealander called Tom Walmsley, who was reading zoology at Bristol University. And last, but not least, there was Janine Booth, whose role as deckhand, whale spotter, lunch packer, agony aunt and nurse made her an invaluable member of the team. It was Janine's job to look after all the whale watchers, or 'patients', as she liked to call us.

The main tool of the research was photography and the aim, over a period of many years, was to build up an identikit picture of every animal seen during the study. A range of other information was being collected as well: dive times, behaviour patterns, water temperature, salinity, and so on.

There were also plans to listen to the minkes on an underwater microphone, to see if they had anything interesting to say. But so far in the project they seemed to be keeping fairly quiet and, besides, the sea was too noisy. Scallop dredgers, in particular, made a din that could be heard for several miles and, even on the rare occasions when they were silent, it was more common to hear submarines gossiping to one another than it was to pick up talking whales; on a bad day underwater around Mull, it must have been comparable to living next to a busy motorway.

Richard explained that this was the only behavioural work being conducted on whales in Britain. The study area was relatively small (between Iona in the south, Tiree in the west, Mull in the east and Rhum in the north) but it was proving to be an excellent place to look for minkes.

Our task for the week was simple: we had to find as many whales as we could, photograph their distinguishing features and then record all their personal details. Nothing could have been easier. Or so we thought.

It rained only twice during the week: once for three days and once for four days. Mull has a fairly high rainfall at the best of times, but I think we must have been witness to at least half of its annual allowance. It was lashing against the windows, overflowing from the gutter, running down the road in torrents and swelling a profusion of puddles around the Lodge. A minke whale would have disappeared from sight if it had fallen into the fathomless pool of water that was forming immediately below my bedroom window.

It was frustrating, to say the least. I crawled out of bed each morning, just before seven o'clock, peered outside at the inevitable downpour and wondered if it was too early to start drinking. Then I wandered down to the common room and joined the others for a listen to the weather forecast, which became something of a daily ritual. The prognosis never improved, of course, but we were always optimistic.

Richard took us out whale watching regardless of the rain, the wind and the choppy seas. He kept his boat in a sheltered anchorage a short walk from the Lodge and, as luck would have it, directly opposite an otter holt. We saw the otters once. There were two of them playing in a rock pool as we waited for Tom to bale out the boat's tender. Someone whispered a loud 'Otter!' and we all stood motionless, hardly daring to breathe, as they splashed and chased one another and rolled around in the pool no more than a hundred yards away. But Tom sneezed and the two animals stopped in their tracks, suddenly aware that they were being watched. They stared back. After a few moments, having regained their composure, they ambled, rather nonchalantly, to a more private playground on the other side of a fallen tree.

Richard's boat was called the *Alpha Beta*, and was about 40 feet long. It made an ideal floating research station. There was a computer on board (linked to a satellite navigation system), a hydrophone and even a couple of voice-activated FM transceivers (which work like walkie-talkies for communicating with people on different parts of the boat).

But the most important piece of equipment was a Mars bar, and Janine's first job of the day was to hang a fresh one from the top of the bridge, where it was in full view of all the patients. It acted as an incentive for everyone to stay sharp-eyed and vigilant: the first person to see a whale won the coveted prize. And it worked. The thought of devouring the bar in front of jealous classmates, and of ending the intolerable *clang... clang... clang...* as it crashed against the bridge roof, was strangely obsessive. It helped us to forget about the wind, the rain, the sea spray, the cold, and the rocking and rolling of the boat, as we weaved our way through a maze of hazardous rocks towards the open sea.

Unfortunately, it soon transpired that there is more to whale research than just keeping sharp-eyed and vigilant. We really had to work for a living, and Janine wasted no time in briefing us on our duties for the day. We were split into two groups of four, placed on alternating one-hour shifts and then assigned individual tasks. One person had to look north

No whales... but still sharp-eyed and vigilant.

and was in charge of the stopclock; one looked south and kept the notes; one looked east and did the photography; and the last one, who looked west, had the job of calling out whatever the whale happened to be doing at the time. Meanwhile, the four people waiting patiently for the second shift made endless pots of coffee.

This was the plan. The moment someone shouted 'whale!' the stopclock expert had to press the appropriate button on the clock, the caller called out what the whale was doing and the notekeeper started taking notes. Then the stopclock expert called out regular time checks, while the caller gave a running commentary and the notekeeper wrote it all down. Meanwhile, the photographer took pictures of anything that moved.

It sounded relatively straightforward – but first we had to find ourselves a whale. Someone had to claim that all-important Mars bar. So to give the patients a fighting chance (after all, we were in direct competition with a crew of professionals) Vassili gave us a brief lesson on minke whale spotting.

Unlike some species, which tend to find the whale watchers first, most minkes require a more determined effort. They are fast swimmers, able to cruise at speeds of 15 miles an hour or more; they have an indistinctive blow that is visible only in the calmest conditions (and never from a distance); they show little of themselves at the surface; and they are far less flamboyant than many of their larger relatives. The trick, Vassili revealed, is to look for any possible sign of activity: a brief glimpse of a fin, a strange splash or even a wave that somehow does not look quite right.

The next part of the lesson was the clock system. This is a tried and tested whale watching trick to ensure that, at a moment's notice, everyone knows where to look for a surfacing whale. For example, if it surfaces over there (to the right) you have to shout 'three o'clock'. If it happens to be over there (to the left) you shout 'nine o'clock'. Over there (immediately behind) would be 'six o'clock', over here (immediately in front) would be twelve o'clock, and so on. We practised a few times until Vassili was certain we could all tell the time satisfactorily.

The third and final part of the lesson was in shouting. This, apparently, is of paramount importance. Like efficient guard dogs, we were trained to shout the moment we saw anything suspicious. If we hesitated, even for a moment, the whale could get away. We were told not to feel embarrassed about making mistakes: no-one would laugh, Vassili assured us, rather unconvincingly.

We had been on the water, bearing up to a light drizzle, for nearly two hours before anything remotely resembling a whale appeared on the scene. It was Janine who spotted it first. In fact, Janine was the only person on board who spotted it at all - and 'it' turned out to be a wave.

She claimed she saw something looking suspiciously like a minke whale's back, between four-thirty and five o'clock and at a distance of several hundred yards. In fact, she saw it twice but no-one else caught a glimpse, even the second time around. It was all a bit suspect (she had been complaining about hunger pangs only a few minutes before) but encouraging nonetheless. For a while, at least, it felt as if there *might* be whales in the vicinity and it was certainly comforting to witness an expert making the first mistake.

Just to be on the safe side, though, we cruised the area until it was time to change shifts, and then slowly made our way further north.

During a shift, no-one was allowed to go to the bathroom without Janine's permission (which she did not grant lightly). But chain-drinking endless cups of coffee was a good enough reason in my book and, as we wended our way towards the Isle of Muck, I was forced to overrule her - and disappeared below deck. I was still there when the inevitable happened. All I heard was someone shouting 'Porpoise! Porpoise!' and a rush of stampeding feet over my head. Apparently, it was right next to the boat but, by the time I emerged, it had disappeared. I know it was nothing to get really upset about, but I could not help myself. What if it was the only sighting we were going to get all week? I questioned the others in the vague, selfish hope that it was nothing more than a fleeting glimpse; at least, I pleaded, tell me that I did not miss a good picture. But, no, they said, the picture opportunities were superb.

I stopped drinking coffee and did not dare go to the bathroom for the remainder of the day. But since there were no more sightings – not even a suspect one – I could have drunk gallons of the stuff without missing a thing.

By the next morning, with no improvement in the weather, the pool of water under my bedroom window had turned into a vast lake; but Richard was desperately trying to be optimistic. Poor Richard. He seemed to feel personally responsible for the vagaries of the Scottish weather. He kept apologising. It was normally beautiful sunshine in the middle of the summer, he assured us, and this was by far the worst week he had experienced in many years. We believed him.

Driving rain reduced visibility to barely the length of the boat. We were making poor headway against a strong northerly wind and the waves were crashing over the bow. Richard decided to stop. With some positive-thinking, and a little luck, he thought there just might be an inquisitive whale nearby that would come and take a closer look. It was a chance in a million, but it had happened before. Minke whales are sometimes extremely curious and, on a number of occasions, have lifted their heads right out of the water next to the *Alpha Beta*. We had even seen photographic evidence of it happening, on one of the walls in the Lodge.

Rather predictably, though, this time there was no inquisitive minke and no lifting of heads. It was becoming glaringly obvious that we were not going to be given whales to watch on a plate.

We were still rolling around on the choppy seas, eating our packed lunches and grumbling about the unfairness of life, when the rain stopped. One minute it was dark and monsoonish, the next the sun was trying to burst through the clouds. Admittedly, the sun shone for no more than an hour, but even that was better than nothing. We could see for 20 or 30 miles in every direction and, for the first time, experienced the spectacular rugged beauty of the Inner Hebrides in all its glory.

It was during this brief lull in the rain that I almost managed to scoop the Mars bar. Far away in the distance was the unmistakable Isle of Eigg which, from the side, looks just like a surfacing humpback whale. It even has a knobbly triangular dorsal fin two-thirds of the way down its back. Optimistically, I pointed this out to Richard but, despite my pleadings and cajolings, he was unimpressed. No chocolate. Absolutely no way. Everyone thought he was being terribly unfair (I had promised to share the bar with the rest of the group) but Richard insisted on waiting until we saw a real whale. We would, he assured us, see one eventually.

Mars bars temporarily forgotten, we cruised past the northern tip of Coll and continued heading vaguely towards Muck. The weather was closing in again when there was a loud ringing sound. It was the phone. I did not even know there was a phone on board and, for a moment, assumed that I was hallucinating. I hate phones with a passion, and have nightmares about them. But it was a microlight pilot, floating somewhere overhead, wanting to talk to Richard. In fact, it was two microlight pilots – Richard Cook and John Boyce – who were flying around the coast of Britain for charity. They had a time limit of two weeks but, thanks to the weather, were already on day four and had barely made a start. They wondered if they could spend the night in the Lodge? Richard agreed and, never one to miss an opportunity, asked if they had seen any whales. The answer was 'no', but they had flown over a small school of dolphins just half an hour before and promised to give us a call if they saw anything bigger.

With two more sharp-eyed and vigilant people on our side, I began to feel more optimistic - especially since the newest members of the team were airborne. Surely, the whales could not escape our notice for much longer? Just to be sure, I wanted to tell Richard and John to look for waves that somehow did not look quite right and to assure them that, if they made a mistake, we would not laugh. But Vassili would not let me.

While everyone else was still looking skyward for microlights, Janine was concentrating on the search for whales. She spotted a party of feeding seabirds, instead. Despite her false alarm the day before, she had eagle-eyes and it was some time before the rest of us could see where she was pointing. As we approached closer the air filled with gannets, kittiwakes, manx shearwaters and lesser black-backed gulls, feeding on a shoal of fish just below the surface. It was a gathering known as a 'hurry' – an apt description since all the birds were frantically wheeling and turning, diving, circling, squabbling and squawking. A hurry, apparently, is a good place to look for minke whales, so we circled the noisy group with our eyes peeled. The birds were going berserk, throwing themselves into the water like hailstones and fighting over scraps of food; we felt sure we would find a minke gorging itself on the hidden feast below. There was even an inquisitive grey seal, which popped its head out of the water several times before swimming underneath the boat and disappearing without trace. But still no whales.

For two more days it rained in torrents. The lake under my bedroom window became an inland sea. The road turned into a river and all the puddles around the Lodge joined forces, lying shoulder to shoulder and leaving a haphazard assembly of stepping-stones for us to hop, skip and jump our way to the main door. But we were determined to see a whale if it killed us and, undaunted by the deluge, continued to go out on the water all day and every day.

Apart from a strange splash that, with a little imagination, looked rather like two minke whales swimming side-by-side, we did not have any luck. But it was worth the effort. We had a superb cream tea on Muck, stopped for a consoling drink or two on Coll, visited a busy colony of puffins on the Treshnish Islands, saw a sea eagle near Rhum and, every evening, watched a small herd of red deer grazing just outside the common room window.

The undisputed highlight was a group of about 30 high-spirited common dolphins that we found somewhere between Mull and Tiree. To be honest, we did not really find them - they found us. They suddenly appeared from nowhere and raced towards the boat, leaping out of the water, riding the waves alongside and then jostling for the best position in front of the bow. Some were swimming just below the surface, within

A common dolphin in high spirits.

inches of the hull, and we could have reached out and touched them. But we just stood there, rising and falling with the waves, soaked through to the skin with sea spray and rain, and watched in awe. The dolphins kept us entertained for a full ten minutes. It was terrific: if we had seen nothing else all week, we would have returned home happy.

We never gave up hope on the whales. Vassili kept us motivated by regaling stories about some of the more memorable sightings from previous trips. We heard tales of so many breaching minkes and feeding orcas that it sometimes seemed as if everyone else on the planet had been to Mull and enjoyed the kind of whale action that we could only dream about. Some groups had so many close encounters on the first day of their holiday that they were feeling quite blasé by the time they had to leave. We did not expect hoardes of whales queuing up to swim around the boat every time we left the anchorage. All we were asking for was one whale. Even a distant one.

At least we knew exactly what we were looking for. We spent every evening in the Lodge drooling over some of the 10,000 minke whale pictures that Richard and Vassili had taken for the project and, after four days, minkes were indelibly imprinted on our brains. We could have recognised one at a hundred paces, with no trouble at all.

Photography was probably the most important part of the project. Every picture had to be compared with all the others, in the hope of finding the same whales more than once. At first glance, they all looked identical but, as Vassili pointed out slight variations in the shapes of their dorsal fins, minor skin blemishes or differences in pigmentation patterns and various scratches and scars, we began to learn how to tell one animal from another. All whales pick up these distinctive marks, from uncomfortably close encounters with orcas, collisions with boats, bites from cookie-cutter sharks and a host of other daily hazards. Unfortunately for the scientists (though not for the whales) the minkes off Mull are not well marked, so individual identification is a very slow, painstaking process. It was a bit like trying to separate portraits of identical twins by minute differences such as individual hairs and moles.

Some of the better-known whales had been given names. There were pictures of them, looking rather like 'Wanted' posters, on one of the walls in the common room: Nick, Groovy, Colgate, Ruth, Chunky, Milli, Stump, Spot, Notch and Nibble. All of them had been named after their most conspicuous features, rather than their characters: Nick had a bite-sized chunk out of the rear side of the dorsal fin, for example, and Groovy had a groove on both sides behind the blowhole. No-one knew whether they were male or female simply because, at sea, it is impossible to tell them apart.

With the help of this photo-identification study, Richard and Vassili have made some exciting discoveries. They know of at least six different minkes (and possibly another four) which return to the waters around Mull every year and always hang around very precise regions within the study area. This may not sound particularly earth-shattering news, but it has some important ramifications for the whaling industry. It suggests that minke whales are not ocean wanderers, as whalers have always assumed, but that they have specific homes. Therefore if a catch quota for, say, the whole of the north-east Atlantic is taken in one particular area, it is likely to have a far greater local impact than anyone had previously thought.

MINKE PATROL –
Scotland

LEFT: *Richard Fairbairns after abandoning the rat-race in favour of a better life far from the madding crowd.*

RIGHT: *Having been trained to look for waves that didn't look quite right, and to shout like efficient guard dogs the moment we saw anything suspicious, all we needed was a whale.*

BELOW: *Common dolphins suddenly appeared from nowhere, raced alongside the boat and then jostled for the best position in front of the bow.*

ABOVE: *A brief moment of excitement as a minke whale surfaces near the boat, winning Richard the coveted Mars bar.*

LEFT AND BELOW: *We consoled ourselves with a superb cream tea on Muck, a drink or two on Coll and a visit to a noisy colony of puffins on the Treshnish Islands.*

THE SWINGIN' HUMPBACKS – **Hawaii**

ABOVE: *What better way to spend a lazy Sunday afternoon than whale watching from the sun-warmed deck of a catamaran, with the Hawaiian island of Maui providing a suitably picturesque backdrop?*

BELOW: *The first time you see a whale break the surface of the water, it can be quite hard to put all the different bumps, bulges and grooves into perspective; this is a humpback whale's head.*

ABOVE: *Look out for a big black Cadillac with a major radiator problem, the on-board naturalist helpfully suggested.*

LEFT: *Whale watching around Hawaii is strictly controlled and many skippers use a rangefinder to maintain the legal distance between them and the whales.*

LEFT: *The humpback whales in Hawaii have more imaginative names than those in many other parts of the world: Amorous Motley, Babe, Ocean Commotion and George IV among them.*

BREACH FROM THE BED – **South Africa**

RIGHT: *Hermanus - the self-proclaimed 'whale capital' of South Africa.*

LEFT: *In South Africa, there is no need to get out of bed in the morning to watch whales .*

RIGHT: *One of the few photographs of a breaching southern right whale ever taken from under the duvet of a hotel bed.*

RIGHT: *One of the female right whales had given birth to a white calf; almost overnight, the town was flooded with TV crews and photographers struggling to capture the new celebrity on film.*

LEFT: *Living in Hermanus is about as close as you can get to having whales in your back garden.*

ABOVE: *Pieter Claasen – the world's first whale crier.*

LEFT: *The 'Whale Route' – a meandering scenic road that makes most other scenic roads seem positively wearisome and boring; here it is skirting along the back of Table Mountain.*

BELOW: *The strange growths, or callosities, on this animal's head are typical of right whales; it's best not to know that they are infested with colonies of barnacles, whale lice and parasitic worms.*

RIGHT: *Although the rock hyrax looks like a guinea pig, by some strange quirk of evolution it is more closely related to elephants and aardvarks.*

Day five was our last full day. It began in a similar vein to the previous four days: heavy rain, a grey, overcast sky and brief spells of optimism from Richard. But this was our last chance to see a whale. This time there would be no changing shifts, no endless cups of coffee, no cream teas on the Isle of Muck – it was all hands on deck or, more appropriately, all eyes on the sea.

We were heading roughly north-west, towards Coll, when Richard had a hunch. By taking into account the tides and currents, and by looking at the sea, sometimes he could guess where the whales might be feeding. Even he did not know how this sixth-sense worked but, apparently, it had been successful too many times to be written off as pure luck. He was well-known for his minke whale hunches, and this was a good one. The bad weather of the past week had not helped but, after an hour or so, the heavy rain miraculously turned to a mere drizzle and Richard looked distinctly confident.

The sea was relatively calm as we zig-zagged our way past the northern tip of Coll. Tom spotted two porpoises and, as we were all watching, a third suddenly appeared no more than 30 yards away. I was glad to be on deck this time, and not locked in the bathroom, although, typically, it was a poor sighting. Harbour porpoises are shy and retiring creatures and generally show little of themselves at the surface: we only saw their low, triangular dorsal fins and a small portion of their dark grey backs. They seemed to roll forward as they dived and the lasting impression was of their fins mounted on revolving wheels that were lifted briefly above the surface and then withdrawn. But we took it as a sign of even better things to come.

We were busy analysing their every move, when the boat swerved violently. There was a muffled conversation coming from the bridge (I think between Vassili and Richard) and, at first, everyone assumed that we must have narrowly missed something in the water. But when Tom came flying up the steps to the observation deck with such a determined look on his face, and armed with his camera, notebook and pen, we knew it was a whale before he had uttered a word.

In all the excitement, everyone abandoned their research stations and the permanent crew were left to the science. We could see the minke about 50 yards away but, like the porpoises, it showed little of itself at the surface. It was hard to tell exactly what was happening. At first, we seemed to be travelling parallel to one another, but then the whale dived and Richard cut the engine. I felt sure that we were getting left behind, but Vassili almost catapulted himself onto the observation deck and told us to look around the boat.

We were straining to see through the drizzle, not quite knowing what to expect, when there was a loud shriek and a blow from the port

A lone shag: one of the many kinds of wildlife we saw that wasn't a whale.

side. The shriek was Janine, the blow was the whale. They both caught us all by surprise and I swung round just in time to see an enormous pointed snout disappearing below the surface, no more than ten yards from where I was standing. I rushed to the other side of the observation deck and almost knocked Janine overboard. She was dashing in the opposite direction, shouting that the whale had dived under the boat and was about to come up on the other side. Leaning over the railings, we watched and waited, anticipating the animal's next move.

Several minutes passed before there was another loud blow, this time from nearer the back of the boat. At first, it sounded like Tom sneezing again, but then I caught a brief, dank smell of cooked cabbage and rotten fish. Minke whales have exceedingly bad breath, and this individual was no exception. As I watched, it lifted its entire head out of the water. Its two outstretched flippers, with their distinctive white 'arm-bands', were completely motionless. They looked like stabilisers on a ship and appeared to be holding the entire animal steady at an angle of about 45 degrees. I breathed in sharply as the whale's tiny eye gave me a long, thoughtful stare and, unprofessionally, forgot to take a single photograph.

Its eye seemed to be so full of acknowledgement, that the best I could do was to stare back.

Its curiosity apparently satisfied, the whale slipped quietly back into the sea. As it sank out of sight, the last we saw was a dark shape slowly growing shadowy and faint, until it vanished altogether. We waited for a full 20 minutes, ever hopeful that it might suddenly reappear. Then Richard emerged from the bridge.

Tom slapped him on the back. One of the patients gave him an enthusiastic 'thumbs up' sign. For a moment, I thought he was going to receive a standing ovation. He was grinning from ear to ear and, although he did not say a word, acknowledged the tributes with a brief nod. Then, in one practised movement, he jumped onto one of the seats in the corner of the observation deck, leaned onto the roof of the bridge and began to untie the Mars bar.

The Swingin' Humpbacks

SINGING HUMPBACK WHALES IN HAWAII

PACIFIC OCEAN

Molokai

Lanai

Lahaina

Maui

Kahoolawe

N

I WAS LYING on the sun-warmed deck of a catamaran, my camera in one hand and an ice cold beer in the other. The sea was the kind of ultramarine blue that you normally find only in holiday brochures and it was so crystal clear that, when I leaned over the side of the boat, I could make out the seabed almost 200 feet below. Behind me was the Hawaiian island of Maui and Haleakala, its 10,000-foot volcano, providing a suitably picturesque backdrop for the last whale watch of the day. I remember thinking: there are worse ways of spending a lazy Sunday afternoon.

Just above my head was a loudspeaker. But there was no blaring music and therefore no irritated couple from Surrey asking the skipper to turn it down. This boat was different. Instead, the air was filled with a baffling medley of moans, groans, roars, snores, squeaks and whistles. Some of the sounds were like the grating of an old metal hinge, others resembled the last gurglings of a drowning man and there was one which could only be described as like the squawking of a chicken with a farmer standing on its toe. In between, there was a beautiful operatic melody that reverberated around the boat and made the hairs on the back of my neck stand on end. We were listening to the plaintive song of a lone humpback whale, eerie in a way but also astonishingly soothing. It had elements of jazz, bebop, blues, heavy metal, classical and reggae all rolled into one. Dozing and meditating in the sun, I could have listened to it all day.

When these unearthly sounds were first heard around the world in the 1970s, thousands of people rushed out to buy recordings of them - making humpback whales the only animals able to boast a top-selling record in the pop charts. But what we were listening to was not a recording. It was the real thing: a haunting and unforgettable live performance. The skipper had dropped an underwater microphone overboard and we were eavesdropping on an unseen whale earnestly singing from somewhere underneath the boat.

The humpback's song is the longest and most complex in the animal kingdom. It may last for half an hour or more. There are usually several main components, which are always sung in the same order but are constantly being refined and improved. This means that the song heard one day is quite different to the one being heard several months later; the entire composition changes over a period of about five years. This remarkable process of reworking and fine-tuning suggests a degree of artistic sensitivity that makes the whales unique. Even the most elaborate bird songs are uniform and unchanging: if a bird suddenly decided to ad-lib, none of its contemporaries would understand what it was saying and in all likelihood it would be doomed to a lonely existence, like an ugly duckling outcast from the rest of the group.

Even more extraordinary is the fact that all the humpbacks in one area sing broadly the same song, incorporating each other's improvisations as they go along. It is as if they write and re-write the music together. Those living in other parts of the world sing very different compositions. They probably all croon about the same trials and tribulations in life, but it is as if the ones living around Hawaii sing in American English, while those living off the coast of Australia, for example, sing in Australian English. The differences are so distinctive that experts can tell where a whale was recorded simply by listening to the intricacies of its own special dialect.

It is only the males that sing. They close their eyes and hang upside-down in the water, heads pointing towards the seabed, and then wave their enormous outstretched flippers up and down like conductors in front of an orchestra. Their aim is to woo their lady loves and to scare away unwanted (and not always gentlemanly) competition. They serenade the females day and night, sometimes repeating their songs over and over again, taking only brief, one-minute pauses for breath.

As we listened to the doleful cries of the whale beneath our boat, a mother and calf were lazily splashing in the water only half a mile from the Maui shoreline. I imagined what it must be like to live in the tall apartment blocks behind them and to wake up every morning to a view of sun, sea and whales, and wondered why I was still living in a corner of the world where people wake up every morning to rain, roads and pigeons. My thoughts were interrupted by a billowing cloud of water vapour as another whale surfaced further to the south. It was far away in the distance but, with the sun disappearing behind the darkening silhouette of Molokai, Maui's neighbour, its blow was brilliant white and stood out against the dimly-lit hillside. I could see it hanging in the still air for a full ten seconds before it faded from view.

The whale beneath the boat was still out of sight, but we could *feel* its presence through the haunting sounds still wafting around the deck. Its song seemed to be full of purpose, as if there was so much to say. In contrast, I had very little to say: words just did not seem to do the song justice. I simply could not think of any suitable adjectives. So I just sat on the deck in silence, quietly contemplating the secrets of the whale's mind and wondering if I could extend my trip by an extra couple of days.

Hawaii is a paradise of year-round sunshine. An archipelago of seven inhabited islands, and many islets and reefs, it stretches out in a 1,600-mile long arc in the middle of the North Pacific – more than 2,000 miles from anywhere.

Its humpback whales are believed to be fairly recent settlers, since there is little evidence of them living in the neighbourhood more than 200 years ago. Where they came from – and why they suddenly moved – is still something of a mystery. But they are obviously fond of the Hawaiian scene: the islands have become a favourite wintering ground for more than half the humpbacks living in the entire North Pacific. They begin to gather there in mid-November and spend the next six or seven months around the islands - wooing, mating and calving – before migrating north to their feeding grounds in the Bering Sea and the Gulf of Alaska. There is little for them to eat in the warm waters of the south and yet their calves could not survive the freezing cold waters of the north – so they have no choice but to lead this nomadic lifestyle.

How they find their way to Hawaii every autumn is another mystery. It takes a skilled navigator to home in on a string of tiny dots in the ocean, especially after swimming across thousands of miles of nothingness or, at least, across thousands of miles of sameness. The earth's magnetic field, temperature gradients, the movement of the sun and stars, ocean currents and a variety of other clues may hold the secret to their pathfinding, but we can only guess at how it all works. The migration route itself is also unknown, despite determined efforts to work it out. The same whales have been photographed in both Hawaii and Alaska many times: it is just what happens during the 3,000-mile journey in between that still needs to be solved. Several animals have been radio-tagged, but all the tags fell off and disappeared within the first week (this was more of a catastrophe than it probably sounds, because each one was worth nearly £4,000). A team of biologists travelled along the most direct route between Hawaii and Alaska and, again, the humpbacks gave them the slip. Then the same team of biologists decided to follow a small family group, but lost them after 600 miles and then did not see a single whale until Alaska; the family of whales was already there when they arrived.

Hawaii has been linked with whales since early in the 19th century, when its central position made it a key player in the Pacific whaling industry. The ports of Honolulu, on the island of Oahu, and Lahaina, on the north-west coast of Maui, were used as staging posts for long whaling expeditions that lasted for three or four years at a time. The whalers hunted sperm whales in a vast expanse of ocean called the 'Japan Grounds', which stretched all the way from north-west Hawaii to near the coast of Japan, and they needed a bolt-hole for brief periods of rest and recuperation. The Hawaiian islands were ideal.

The first whaling ships arrived in 1819 and hundreds of others soon followed in their wake. It was not long before each vessel was rubbing shoulders with a neighbour and, in peak periods during spring and autumn, they filled the two ports to capacity. They transferred their precious cargos to trading ships heading for lucrative markets around the world, made any necessary repairs, stocked up on food and then headed straight back to the whaling grounds until their next visit many months later.

In supplying the needs of the new industry, Honolulu and Lahaina were transformed into goldrush towns although, of course, the 'gold' was whale oil and whalebone. The two ports changed beyond all recognition, becoming much richer but also wilder and more dangerous. After long months at sea, the weather-beaten whalers were interested only in whisky and women and were determined to have a good time. Working on the premise that 'there is no god west of Cape Horn', they let nothing stand in their way and frequently ran amok through the two towns, rioting, shooting, whoring, gambling and drinking. They even had street fights with missionaries who tried to quell their late night revelry.

The whaling industry had been both good and bad for Hawaii. So there were mixed feelings when it started to decline in the late 1850s. In the space of little more than a decade, the whalers had to contend with several insurmountable difficulties that put them on a slippery slope towards extinction. No-one could reverse the trend. The discovery of petroleum, in 1859, caused a drop in the value of whale oil; years of intensive hunting made the whales scarcer and much harder to find; and the supply of ships was adversely affected by the Civil War in North America. The death blow finally came in 1871 when almost the entire North Pacific whaling fleet was destroyed by an early Arctic freeze – and the flow of whalers stopped altogether.

Staggeringly, the humpbacks living around Hawaii managed to survive the wild whaling days relatively unscathed. Thousands upon thousands of whalers passed through their breeding grounds every year, but they were more interested in the nightly fun and games on shore; and, fortunately, they knew that humpbacks produce a rather inferior oil. The islanders themselves established several shore-based whaling stations, between 1840 and 1870, but they never really liked whale meat and had trouble drumming up much enthusiasm for their work. In fact, they had so little success that, every time they killed a whale, it made front page headlines in the local press.

Elsewhere in the North Pacific, commercial hunting of humpbacks began in earnest in 1910 and continued for many years; during the Second World War, American bombers even used the hapless animals for target practice. By the time they received full international protection, in 1966, their numbers had plummeted from around 15,000 to fewer than 1,000 and they were on the verge of extinction.

No-one really knows how many humpbacks survive in the North Pacific today. There may be as many as 3,000 – with a major proportion of them breeding around Hawaii – but even this is merely a fraction of the original population. The one certainty is that they are still in such a precarious situation that they may never fully recover.

'Look out for a big black Cadillac with a major radiator problem', the on-board naturalist helpfully suggested. He was trying to explain what a humpback whale looks like to a group of men lounging around in the back of the boat. Unfortunately, it was a group of decidedly uninterested men, who were doing more lounging than listening. Engrossed in a rather convoluted discussion about the traffic in New York, the weather in

A humpback whale dives off the coast of Maui.

Nebraska and the best place to buy chocolate-chip ice cream in Seattle, they did not take a blind bit of notice. Even when an underwater microphone was dropped overboard and the haunting sounds of a singing whale interrupted their incessant jabbering, they paused for no more than a brief moment before commencing a swap of baseball caps to see who had the biggest head. Then they yelled over to the skipper and demanded to have the radio turned on instead: the 'wailing', they complained, was worse than 'a goddamn dentist's drill'.

Hawaii was full of whale watchers who seemed emphatically indifferent to the whales and it was a mystery how some of them came to be on the boats at all. I wondered if, back home in New York, Nebraska or Seattle, they had a habit of buying tickets to football matches when they did not really like football, or forced themselves to sit through late-night movies when all they really wanted to do was to prop up all-night bars. The irony is that they probably did not *intend* to go whale watching at all. I expect they were abducted by the hoardes of whale watching touts who gather along Front Street, in the old whaling port of Lahaina, and hard-sell the whales to anyone who happens to be passing within earshot. To be fair, of course, these touts are about as closely related to the whale watch operators as trinket sellers in front of Saint Peter's are related to the Pope. But they can be very persuasive. Even passers-by who had planned never to see a whale in their lives are pestered into changing their minds and suddenly find themselves standing on the deck of a whale watch boat, heading out to sea, before they fully realise what has happened.

But if you *do* want to see a whale, Front Street is one of the few places in the world where it is possible to go shopping for a suitable trip simply by wandering along the seafront and seeking out the best price, the right departure time and the most comfortable boat. It faces the largest humpback breeding grounds in the North Pacific and has become the centre of Hawaii's whale watching industry, attracting more than 100,000 people every year. There is a confusing mishmash of trips on offer. Some focus on the whales, some on the sailing, several combine whale watching with snorkelling, candlelit dinners or sunset cruises, and between them they have a motley collection of vessels, from yachts and catamarans to rigid-hulled inflatables and even a boat with a glass bottom. It is an impossible choice: if you believe everything you are told along Front Street, every trip is the ultimate, unrivalled, world-beating whale watch experience.

I experimented with many of the operators and found only one common ingredient: everyone stuck religiously to the letter of the law. Whale watching around Hawaii is more strictly controlled than in most other parts of the world and the Hawaiian authorities are determined that it will not add to umpteen hazards that the humpback whales already have to tolerate on their breeding grounds.

Imagine how you would feel if there was a constant stream of private boaters and inter-island ferries passing through your lounge, low-flying aircraft continuously hovering at your bedroom window, a flood of agricultural chemicals over your bathroom floor, new shops and hotels being constructed on your doorstep and regular military manoeuvres in your hall. Then add 100,000 complete strangers sitting at one end of your bed, hidden in cupboards, perched on the staircase and sliding down the bannisters, all talking loudly in foreign languages and taking photographs of your every move. The chances are it would scupper your private life. You might even be tempted to move house (assuming, of course, that there was another one ready and waiting for you to occupy).

The gist of the whale watching regulations is that it is illegal to get too close. If a whale wants to be friendly, and has a sudden urge for a face-to-face encounter, that is fine; some whales are like that. But if a boat makes the first approach, the skipper is likely to get into very serious trouble. Hawaiian law states that in areas where most of the humpbacks congregate (which is in Maalaea Bay and within two miles of Lanai) it is illegal to approach them closer than 300 yards; elsewhere in Hawaiian waters, up to the 100-fathom contour, it is illegal to go within 100 yards. There is a $25,000 fine for anyone who breaks the law – and it seems to work. Some of the skippers leave nothing to chance and cut their engines at 400 or 500 yards, while others use rangefinders to measure the distances more accurately.

This law may be good for the whales, but there is no denying that it can be rather frustrating for the whale watchers. I may have been particularly unlucky but I did not have a single close encounter with a humpback in Hawaii - although I had a great many sightings on almost every trip. The whales must come first, of course, but I could never understand why there was so much emphasis on watching them from afar and so little on their singing. After all, there are not many places in the world where, at the drop of a microphone, you can almost guarantee spontaneous attendance at a live humpback whale concert. Yet sometimes we were treated to no more than a brief soupçon of a song and, once in a while, were not given the opportunity to listen at all. It was akin to attending a Rolling Stones concert – and then sitting in the back row, where it is impossible to make out any detail of the tiny figures on stage, and being forced to wear ear plugs for the entire performance.

It was not always the fault of the operators. Some did focus on the songs and interpreted them with entertaining commentaries about the singers and their amorous intentions. But like the baseball cap-wearers from New York, Nebraska and Seattle, many of their clients seemed to be a little brain-dead; or, to be more precise, their part of the brain that makes most normal people take an interest in the things around them seemed to be missing. Admittedly, listening to a singing humpback whale is not everyone's idea of a good time, but it does take a special kind of person to find it less interesting (even for five minutes) than a verbal evaluation of chocolate-chip ice cream shops or a competition to see who has the biggest head.

The whales in Hawaii have more imaginative names than those in most other parts of the world. After a few days, the list of sightings in my notebook was beginning to read like a list of favourites for the Grand National, combined with a selection of possible titles for a new rock album. It included Amorous Motley, Gurgle, Jay Jay, Ocean Commotion, Chace Dillon, George IV, Winkle, Babe, Crossbite, Hokulele (which means 'shooting star') and Uilani (meaning 'heavenly beauty') just for starters. A passenger on one trip suggested that it was because Hawaiians grow stronger marijuana than anyone else, though I doubt if that is the real reason. It is probably more to do with the famous 'Aloha!' spirit, which encourages a more relaxed, easy-going attitude than people in most other parts of the world could muster on their days off. Hawaiians are so laid-back they walk around on their shoulder blades.

I spent several days adding new sightings to my list in the company of the Pacific Whale Foundation. A non-profit organisation, founded in 1980, the PWF operated three different boats for whale watching: a 53-foot motor vessel, a 50-foot sailing ketch and a 65-foot catamaran. Its on-board naturalists were eminently well-informed and provided outstanding commentaries, especially compared to some of the ones I had heard earlier in the week which, at best, were both trivial and inaccurate. They even handed out free Whale Watching Guides and organised weekly slide presentations at some of the local hotels. There was a strong conservation message in all their work and, since they had reached more than a quarter of a million people already, their whale watching operation was clearly making a significant contribution to raising levels of awareness about humpback whales and their uncertain future.

Like most of the Front Street operators, the Pacific Whale Foundation guarantees sightings. The chances of paying for a trip and not seeing the featured attraction are virtually nil – the PWF has a 99.6 per cent success rate – but, if you are incredibly unlucky, and the whales fail to appear, you receive a 'Just a Fluke' coupon for a free trip another day.

I was lucky and saw whales on every trip. In fact, I saw umpteen whales on every trip. Like London buses, Hawaiian humpbacks tend to come along in twos and threes and, often, there would be as many as 15 or 20 in sight at any one time.

One day I saw a group of five together. Four hot-blooded males suddenly started harassing an unfortunate female, as she minded her own business a few hundred yards from the boat. In a moment, the female was making a dash for safety while the males, strung out in a line behind her, were squabbling and jostling for prime position next to their potential mate. They head-butted one another, pushed and shoved like crowds of people swarming into the first day of a Harrods sale –

and rapidly dispelled the myth of the 'gentle giant'. There was so much splashing, and so many bodies rolling around in the water, that it was impossible to tell if the female finally succumbed.

Other unattached females had clearly experienced similar goings-on the year before and, by the time I saw them, had become mothers with young calves. When they are first born, humpback whales are about 14 feet long and weigh more than a ton. Producing one must be like giving birth to a VW Beetle. But, like many aspects of a humpback whale's private life, it is a feat that has yet to be witnessed. It is not exactly something you could miss (it would be like failing to notice a rhinoceros fall out of a tree) but, so far, no-one happens to have been underwater in the right place at the right time.

I contented myself with listening to another song from underneath the boat as we drifted, barely a mile offshore, with a hydrophone in the water. This time, there seemed to be two singers, one very close (it sounded as if it was in the bridge with the skipper) and the other, barely audible, far away in the distance.

So many impressions kept crowding in on me but, most of all, I was overwhelmed by a sense of the unknown. I realised that if I had been eavesdropping on a conversation between two little green men on Mars I would have been little further from being able to decipher what they were saying. The intriguing but inescapable fact is that we are only just beginning to understand these extraordinary forms of intelligent life on our own planet. As one Hawaiian whale researcher put it, after decades of research our knowledge has progressed from almost nothing to a little bit.

Breach from the Bed

RIGHT WHALES FROM A HOTEL BED IN SOUTH AFRICA

SOUTH AFRICA

Cape Town

Fish Hoek

Cape of
Good Hope

Hermanus

Walker Bay

Danger Point

Cape Agulhas

ATLANTIC OCEAN

N

FORGET SEASICKNESS, stormy weather, crowded boats and rising at the crack of dawn. In South Africa, you do not even have to get out of bed in the morning to watch whales.

This is what you do. Check in to a comfortable hotel overlooking the sea: it is not necessary to have a balcony, but it is important to push your bed right up against the window. Before you turn in for the night, set your alarm for about eight o'clock. As soon as you wake up, call room service and order a piping hot cup of tea and some biscuits. Then all you have to do is to sit up in bed, drink the tea, eat the biscuits and watch the whales that will be swimming around outside your bedroom window. You may have to clamber out of bed briefly to draw back the curtains but, otherwise, no special fitness or skills are required.

The whales you will be looking at are southern right whales, which enter bays and inlets along the South African coast every southern winter. They start arriving in large numbers during June and stay for several months to mate, calve and, in the case of a few unfortunate non-breeders, simply to grow another year older. They begin to leave sometime in late October.

The last one to go is a legendary whale called Wendy. According to local folklore, every year it is her job to round up the other whales and to make sure they are all safely on their way. She turns out the light, metaphorically speaking, and disappears herself some time during the third week in November.

No-one knows where all the whales go: they just disappear and that is the last anyone sees of them until the following winter. But there is growing evidence to suggest that they head for an area south of their breeding grounds, in colder waters near the Antarctic. This is where they feed, on high densities of tiny crustaceans called copepods. It is a long way to have to swim for a good meal but, unfortunately, the whales have no choice: the Antarctic waters have plenty of food but are too cold and exposed for baby whales; on the other hand, the South African waters are warm and protected but have no food. So the entire population has to swim backwards and forwards every year between their breeding grounds in the north and their feeding grounds in the south.

Until quite recently, few southern right whales were seen at any time of the year and it was possible to lie in bed for weeks, or even months, without a single sighting. After centuries of intensive whaling, there were few of them left: the species was virtually extinct.

The southern right whale, and its close relative the northern right whale, were the first large whales to be commercially exploited. So-named because they were considered the 'right' whales to catch, they were slow-moving, rich in oil and baleen, and obligingly floated on the water after they had been harpooned. Whalers in the Bay of Biscay were hunting them as early as the 11th century and, in the years to come, they became one of the most ruthlessly hunted of all the world's whales.

In South Africa, so many were killed in their breeding bays along the coast that, by the time they were given international protection, in 1935, there were probably no more than 25 breeding females left. It was a similarly depressing story in other parts of the world.

Somehow, since the end of the whaling era, the southern right whale has made a remarkable recovery. Its population now stands at around 5,000 worldwide and is still increasing by about seven per cent every year. More than 1,600 of these whales live in southern Africa, with similar numbers in South America and Australia and several hundred dotted around other parts of the southern hemisphere. They are not safe yet - current populations are still a mere fraction of their original levels - but, with careful protection, their future is looking more secure than it has done for many years.

This is one reason why South Africa has the strictest whale protection laws in the world. No-one is allowed to approach a whale closer than about 300 yards (watching the animals by boat is actively discouraged) and anyone who disobeys the strictly-enforced law risks a hefty fine of R5,000 or up to six years imprisonment, or both.

The situation is simple - if you want to watch whales in South Africa, you have to watch them with your feet firmly on the ground. This may sound frustrating, or even downright implausible: whale watching from dry land probably seems about as hopeless as bird watching from the bottom of the sea. But South Africa's whales come so near to shore that, by sitting on a well-chosen rock, or by languishing in a well-chosen bed, it is possible to have an even closer encounter across the habitat barrier than it is from a boat in many other parts of the world.

I was driving along the 'Whale Route', a meandering scenic road that makes most other scenic roads seem positively wearisome and boring. Hugging the South African coastline, from the Atlantic to the Indian Ocean, it starts in Cape Town, skirts along the back of Table Mountain, ambles around the Cape of Good Hope and then twists and turns its way to the southernmost tip of the continent and beyond. It is the kind of road that makes you stop every few miles to gasp, or to contemplate the meaning of life. Every time you turn a corner, another paintable seascape comes into view and a little voice in your head tells you to record it for posterity. Unfortunately, I could not paint a picture to save my life, so I snapped photographs instead, and stopped at frequent intervals to commit the best excerpts of the journey to memory. I can still close my eyes and conjure up images of mountains, sky, sea and sand, and dream my way along every inch of that unforgettable road.

As its name suggests, the Whale Route was intended more for whales than for its dazzling scenery. To be more precise, it was intended primarily for whale watchers. There are official whale viewing sites dotted every few miles along the coast, where it is possible to pull off the road and watch whales in the same way that, in other parts of the world, you can pull off the road and buy hamburgers.

The first whale viewing site I encountered was just outside the Cape of Good Hope Nature Reserve. The place was deserted (I had not seen another car for miles) apart from a sprinkling of Hartlaub's gulls. Like bored commuters waiting for a train, the gulls were pacing around beneath a sign that showed a picture of a whale spouting.

To avoid raising my hopes, and then having them dashed, I had already convinced myself that I would not see a whale. And sure enough, I didn't. I scanned the vast expanse of False Bay through my binoculars: a pied crow, a white-breasted cormorant, some more gulls, a distant fishing boat, a couple of rocks and a piece of floating seaweed. But no whales.

The kind of view that makes you stop every few miles to gasp.

I was not surprised. After all, it did seem a little unlikely that there would be one at the appointed place – especially as it had to be there, ready and waiting, at the precise moment that I happened to pull off the road. In Florida, you do not expect to see an alligator lying next to a sign that says 'Gators Crossing'; and, in England, the signs showing a deer ballet dancing generally guarantee that you will not see a deer, let alone one doing a *grand jeté*.

So I was just beginning to wonder whether the analogy with buying a hamburger was rather optimistic when, out of the corner of my eye, I glimpsed a movement in the water. I swung around just in time to see one of the rocks disappear below the surface. As I watched, the other rock grew wider, and longer, and suddenly sprouted an enormous head. It breathed a V-shaped blow into the air, rolled briefly to one side, and then dropped from sight. I quickly checked the floating seaweed, and the distant fishing boat, in case they had metamorphosed as well (they had not) and then waited for the whales to reappear.

A few moments later, they surfaced and blew in unison: it was a mother and her calf. They were so close to shore that, from my vantage point next to the road, I could discard the binoculars and still make out every little detail of their heads and backs. The whale viewing site was on a small cliff, about 50 feet from the sea, and the two animals were almost directly below me. Lolling around in the water together, they were unaware of being watched and seemed to feel safe and secure in the protected South African waters. The sight of them relaxing together, completely undisturbed, brought a lump to my throat.

Like all southern right whales, these two did not have dorsal fins. Their backs were jet black, their bodies smooth and rotund, and they floated higher in the water than any other whale I had seen. The mother was enormous. I guessed she was almost 50 feet long and so wide that the visible portion of her back was virtually round; she resembled a half-submerged hot-air balloon. But there was still something about her that screamed 'Whale!', like a sixth-sense telling me to look more closely. I promised myself that I would not mention mistaking her for a rock to anyone.

The calf was an exact replica of its mother, though only about a third of her length. It never ventured far from her side – rarely more than a few feet, in fact – but was in a boisterous mood and seemed to be desperate for some attention. It nudged her a few times, slapped her on the back with its tail and then rubbed snouts. But its efforts were wasted and, after a while, it settled down for an incontestably quiet morning in the shallows.

As I waited for something else to happen, I noticed a second sign at the whale viewing site. In fact, I had been leaning against it for some time. This one warned unwary travellers about baboons. 'Warning', it said. 'Baboons are dangerous. Picnic and stop at your own risk'. There were no baboons in sight, but I had heard about their habit of loitering along the roadside: they try not to look dangerous but, nevertheless, loiter with intent.

South African baboons know all about whale watching. They know that, if there is a car coming and a whale spouting, the car will pull into the viewing site, the driver and all the passengers will jump out and then, for a few precious moments, all the doors will be left invitingly open. While the whale watchers watch the whale, they themselves are being watched by a 'lookout baboon' and their car is being ransacked by the other members of the gang.

Coming from southern England, I am rather neurotic about thefts from cars and have a habit of locking all the doors, even if I am standing less than three feet away. But I did not bargain for baboon ingenuity and gall. As I was watching the whales, I suddenly had a strange feeling of being watched myself and turned around to see two baboons sitting on the bonnet of my car, desperately trying to yank off the windscreen wipers. There was another tugging at the offside wing mirror and a fourth bending the aerial backwards and forwards, waiting patiently for it to snap. Overseeing the robbery from the roof was a huge male, looking like a Wimbledon umpire presiding over an important Centre Court tennis match.

We froze and stared at one another in disbelief. The smaller baboons looked rather embarrassed, like juvenile delinquents caught smoking behind the bike shed. But the huge male muttered something under his breath and, obediently, five pairs of eyes gave me a disdainful look that said: 'Oh yeah, and what are you going to do about it?'. My brain was still deciding how I should deal with the situation, when the smallest baboon sneezed; unaccountably, this caused the aerial to keel over and clatter onto the ground. In an instant, fear overcame belligerence and, in one coordinated movement, the entire gang bounded into the bushes carrying various parts of my hire car under their arms and on their heads.

I had visions of them stealing the spare tyre, a couple of hubcaps and perhaps the number-plates from the next vehicle that happened to stop at the viewing site. Lurking in the bushes were the makings of a brand new car of their own.

Later in the day, I stopped at another whale viewing site on the outskirts of Fish Hoek, overlooking False Bay, and had problems with a different kind of primate. This time it was a huge male motorcyclist wearing a crash helmet with a darkened visor. All I could see of his face was the end of a straggly ginger beard, which wiggled as he tried to sell me a car sticker saying 'Give me hugs instead of drugs'. I explained that it was a hire car, and that I could not put a sticker on it, but all the hire cars he had ever seen were fully-equipped with windscreen wipers and aerials, so he did not believe me. I bought a sticker anyway, in the hope that he might go away.

He did not. Having taken my 10 Rand, he proceeded to tell me everything he knew about whales, which was rather little. As if passing on classified information, he divulged that right whales have the largest penises in the world (which is true), that these can measure up to eight feet long (which is also true) and, most important of all, he told me, they use them like baseball bats to attack fishing boats (which, of course, is not true). By way of a demonstration, he began to swing one of his arms around wildly.

I was in the middle of a hasty retreat when he noticed the number-plate on the back of the car. To the uninitiated, PZH 712T probably seems quite harmless, but beardie went beserk. He called me all the names under the sun for refusing to let him remove the offending article and throw it into the sea. He left, eventually, but only after I had promised to mention it to the car hire company. They did not know what he was talking about, either.

The heart of the Whale Route is a town called Hermanus. The self-proclaimed 'whale capital' of South Africa, Hermanus sprawls along a narrow coastal plateau between the Klein River mountains and Walker Bay. It is a popular seaside resort, just a couple of hours drive from Cape Town (or, if you take the long way round, which I did, a couple of days drive from Cape Town).

Hermanus retains the character and charm of a small village. Even during the summer, when its population trebles from 11,000 to more than 30,000, there is a pleasant and welcoming atmosphere about the place. It is home to a motley collection of houses, several churches, a few grand old hotels, a railway station (but no railway line) and some sensational views. Wherever you stand in the town, you can see either the mountains, or the sea, or both.

There is a ferocious storm that hits the Hermanus area once in a while. It is called the *Sewedaereen*, or Seven Day Rain. Appropriately, it lasts for seven days. And, strangely enough, it hits roughly once every seven years, so it could have been called the Seven Year Rain. It is a rare event simply because it requires very specific weather conditions to gain momentum: precisely the right amount of wind, the correct temperature, and so on.

Against all the odds, the *Sewedaereen* hit Hermanus on exactly the same day that I did. When I checked into the hotel, there was no hint of the storm to come: the sun was shining and the air was stiflingly hot. By the time I had showered and unpacked my shorts and T-shirts and suntan lotion, there was a welcoming sea breeze. Some hours later, when I turned in for the night, the breeze had whipped itself into a bluster and the sea was beginning to look uninvitingly storm-tossed. And by morning, the wind was howling around the balcony and rattled the panes of glass in the patio doors like a demented window cleaner.

I ventured outside, briefly, and came back in. It was raining hard. To describe the rain as a heavy downpour would not do the *Sewedaereen* sufficient justice. The hotel manager described it as a heavy sidepour, because it was not just raining – it was doing it horizontally. And the wind was so strong it turned the raindrops into bullets.

I returned to my room, called room service and crawled back into bed. The wind had created a vortex inside the balcony where, for a bit of variety, it was actually raining upwards. I stared out of the window. Not a whale in sight. I had been told that they move farther offshore in bad weather and I wondered how they were coping with the heavy seas that were barely discernible in the grey murk below the horizon.

I stayed in bed all day, feeling sorry for myself, and for the whales. Sunday yawned into Monday and, after a brief recce as far as the front door of the hotel, I decided to stay put. In fact, to be honest, I stayed in bed for most of the week. It was pointless going outside - I could barely stand up in the wind and the roads were all flooded - so the days passed slowly. Then one morning the rain stopped and the wind died. The *Sewedaereen* was no more. It disappeared just like that: exactly seven days after we had both arrived in town.

The next day, the whales were back in force, and with them was a minor celebrity. One of the females had given birth to a white calf. Crowds of people lined up along the harbour wall, commenting on the sensational contrast between the calf's brilliant white skin, speckled with black, and the dark skin of its mother. Most right whales have at least some white markings (especially on the underside) but near-albinos are exceedingly rare and, by the end of the week, Hermanus was brimming with TV crews and photographers struggling to capture it on film. The baby whale was seen by millions of people around the world and, almost overnight, it kickstarted the local economy with an unexpected, but most welcome, mini-tourist boom. Hermanus was well and truly on the whale watcher's map.

Living in Hermanus is about as close as you can get to having whales in your back garden. There are many local people, with houses along the coast, who can sit and watch them cavorting in the bay while the rest of us watch starlings squabbling on the bird table. There may be several dozen whales within sight of the lounge, or the kitchen sink, or the bedroom, at any one time.

These people are proud of their whales and make strenuous efforts to show them to visitors. For a start, they have prepared a wonderful clifftop path – reputedly the best whale watch walk in the world – which gives whale watchers a grandstand view. Stretching all the way from the New Harbour, at one end of town, to the mouth of the Klein River lagoon, at the other, it covers a total of nearly eight miles. You can settle down on a rock, or on one of many strategically-placed wooden benches, and enjoy the sea breeze, smell the scent of kelp, watch distant breakers crashing onto jagged rocks, and share a pleasant day with the whales.

If, for any reason, the whales are not forthcoming, there is always help at hand. Every winter and spring, twice a day, seven days a week, when the whales are in town, Hermanus echoes to the deep bass sound of a kelp horn. It is blown by Pieter Claasen, the world's first whale crier. Pieter's job is to alert locals and visitors to the most recent whale sightings. Wearing a Robin Hood costume complete with perky hat, he is impossible to miss. Doing his rounds in the centre of town, at ten o'clock every morning and three o'clock every afternoon, he blows an ear-splitting coded message that reveals the exact location of the nearest animals. For the benefit of visitors, who are rarely able to decipher the code, he has all the information written on a sandwich board, and provides a free map, directions and a profusion of additional information as well.

The whale crier is more than a tourist gimmick: the locals are genuinely interested in his twice-daily announcements. Although they see whales all the time, watching them is like watching a TV soap opera. It becomes addictive.

Every evening, after work, many of them park their cars at a place called Gearings Point. Some take a picnic, or a flask of coffee, others just sit and gaze at the wide, sweeping views of Walker Bay, quietly watching the whales in the fading light. What better way to wind down after a hard day at the office? Even though I was spending a lot of time watching whales from my hotel bed, and not really working at all, I quickly fell into the same regular habit.

One day, I was sitting alone on the rocks just below the Point, warm and cosy in the late afternoon sun. I was surrounded by rock dassies. These curious rodent-like animals look suspiciously like oversized guineapigs but, by some strange quirk of evolution, are more closely related to elephants and aardvarks. I felt sorry for them because every time I moved – even if I just scratched my nose – they panicked and went scuttling for cover. They always reappeared a few seconds later, but never mustered enough courage to stay put long enough to make it worth their while.

I was trying to watch a whale take a leisurely evening swim. It was a little way down the coast, but no more than a few yards from shore, and kept rolling onto its back to wave a flipper in the air. If whales could stroll, that is exactly what it was doing. Gradually, it made its way past the Old Harbour entrance until it was next to me and my rock. Every time it blew I was showered in the wet, smelly spray of its cabbagey breath: it brought a whole new meaning to being within spitting distance. At one point, the huge animal was so close that I could have stepped off the rock and straight onto its back.

As it moved away, the whale gave me a quick, sideways glance and, for a brief moment, I had a magnificent close-up view of the 'callosities' on its head. These strange growths are typical of right whales and first appear when they are very young. Each individual whale can be recognised by the unique pattern of callosities. Made of keratin (which is the principal ingredient of rhino horn and human finger nails) their function is unclear, but one theory is that they form a 'splash guard' to stop water getting into the blowholes.

Most callosities are infested with colourful, albeit rather unpleasant, colonies of barnacles, whale lice and parasitic worms. They occur on the chin, on the sides of the head, above the eyes, on the lower lips, and near the blowholes. But the largest of them all sits right on the top of the whale's head. This one is called the 'bonnet' because, apparently, it resembles a woman's hat. The zoologist who named it must have been blind, or drunk, or both, because I have never seen a woman wearing a hat anything like it. And I am sure I would have remembered if I had.

There was a restaurant in Hermanus, near Gearings Point, called The Burgundy. Located in a fisherman's cottage, with fabulous views of the Bay, it was reputed to be one of the best places to eat in the whole of South Africa. Its proprietor was Michael Olivier, a delightful and jovial man, with the patience of *Job*. He needed it.

The first time I ate in The Burgundy, I was just being served a heaped bowl of *moules marinieres* when there was an incredibly loud splash outside. It sounded as though a car had rolled off Gearings Point into the sea just beyond the Old Harbour wall. But someone shouted 'Whale!' and, for a split second, the restaurant fell silent. We all stopped what we were doing, and looked up: one of the waiters was frozen in a crouching position, with a corkscrew in his hand and a bottle of wine between his legs; a lady on the table next to me had a spoonful of *crêpes suzette* hovering in front of her mouth; and an old man with a streaming cold held a handkerchief to his nose, in the middle of a blow.

We must have been communicating by telepathy because, without a word being uttered, the entire restaurant suddenly scrambled for the door. It was as if someone had clicked their fingers and called 'Action!'. We bolted towards the harbour, some still with glasses of wine and cutlery in their hands, others munching mouthfuls of food. One man had a pink serviette tucked into his trousers.

I glanced over my shoulder and saw Michael slap his knee with delight. A waiter was standing at the window with a plate of food in each hand; his jaw was hanging open.

Several cars had stopped in the middle of the road and people were pouring down the steps towards the water. As I came to the War

Memorial, overlooking the bay, I looked down towards the crowd that was gathering on the harbour wall. No more than 50 yards beyond them was a whale – in mid-air. I hurtled down the harbour steps as it disappeared below the surface and watched as it breached again. By the time I launched myself onto the wall I was moving so fast that I lost control and almost knocked a small boy headlong into the water. The whale breached again.

We watched, and gasped, and cheered together for a full ten minutes. It was the most incredible display of breaching I had ever seen. There was just one thing missing: my camera. All I had with me was a knife with a knob of butter on the end. I cursed myself for being so unprofessional and wrestled with my conscience – should I run back to the hotel for the equipment, or should I stay and watch? I resolved to stay and watch. I think it was the right decision.

When the show was over, the crowd dispersed and we returned to wait for our meals to be re-heated and to toast 'the breacher' with several bottles of local wine. I returned to the hotel in jocular mood.

That night, I went to sleep with the windows wide open, lying in the moonlight and listening to another whale blowing in the bay below.

I awoke to loud coughings and wheezings. It sounded like a heavy smoker clearing his throat, in the middle of an asthma attack, while drowning. I later heard it described as a cross between a baby elephant trumpeting and a lion roaring. Suffice to say that it was one of the strangest sounds I have ever heard. I sat up in bed and looked out of the window: the 'culprits' were two whales that were rolling around in the surf, no more than a hundred yards away.

It is a great mystery how right whales, and some other species, can venture so close to shore without stranding. Many whales are unable to cope with shallow water and, every year, hundreds of them strand and die on beaches all over the world. Yet the right whales around Hermanus habitually enter shallow water with no trouble at all. The last stranding was in 1989 but, even then, the animal had probably died at sea and was washed ashore with the tides and currents. There are plans to excavate its skeleton for a new whale museum although, unfortunately, the body has been mislaid (after all, it was only about 50 feet long and weighed in the region of 80 tons). Everyone remembers burying it, on a wide stretch of beach on the outskirts of town, but no-one remembers exactly where. The Rotary Club organised a fund-raising event to find the missing body.

Plots on the beach were sold for 5 Rand apiece and hundreds of people spent a day digging, but the whale remained well and truly hidden.

I called room service for my customary tea and biscuits, and settled down for a pleasant morning's whale watch. I had a wide, sweeping view from the bed and counted a total of 18 different whales from one end of Walker Bay to the other. There were so many, I did not know where to look next.

Beyond the two in the shallows, towards Danger Point, there were three more swimming along in single file. Another seemed to be standing on its head, motionless, with just its tail showing above the surface, and its nearest neighbour was waving a broad, paddle-shaped flipper in the air. Further out, in the distant reaches of the bay, a lone whale was breaching. I could hear the sound of it hitting the water, even though I was tucked up in bed nearly a mile away. It hurled itself high into the air, arched its back and, as it smashed into the sea, sent up a wall of spray on either side.

Room service arrived. I sat up in bed. Munching a chocolate biscuit, with a cup of tea in one hand and binoculars in the other, I watched the distant whale breach 14 times more.

What is the rest of the world doing today? I wondered. I would not have swapped places with anyone.

Appendices

GUIDELINES FOR WHALE WATCHING

W<small>ATCHING WHALES</small> should be an eyes-on-hands-off activity. It is sometimes easy to forget that we are uninvited guests in their world - that we are privileged to see them. We have a responsibility to cause as little disturbance as possible and, more than that, to help them benefit from whale watching through education, fund-raising, research and a variety of other closely-related activities.

The golden rule is always to consider the safety and welfare of the whales before attempting to watch them. Without due care and attention, the noise and movement of boats can be unnecessarily stressful and, of course, there is always the risk of propellers causing serious injury.

In many parts of the world there are strict regulations for whale watching and it is important to be familiar with these before heading out to sea. But, in the meantime, here are some simple dos and don'ts:

Do...
*   approach slowly (never faster than idle or 'no wake' speed)
*   approach from a position parallel and slightly to the rear
*   position the boat at least 1,000 feet ahead of travelling whales (though not directly in their path) and wait for them to approach you
*   move away if there is another boat already within 300 feet of a whale
*   stay a sensible and safe distance away from particularly active whales
*   take special care around calves
*   keep the engine in neutral if a whale approaches the boat, and allow it to idle for about a minute before switching off
*   move away slowly (never faster than idle or 'no wake' speed)
*   move away if you notice any signs of distress, such as a rapid change in direction or speed, prolonged diving or underwater exhalation

Do not...
*   approach closer than 100 feet
*   attempt a head-on approach
*   separate or scatter a group of whales
*   cut off their path or try to chase or drive whales in a particular direction
*   travel faster than the slowest whale in a group
*   make sudden changes in speed or direction
*   make loud noises
*   stay near a whale for longer than 15 minutes
*   re-engage the propellers until you see the whale at the surface and are certain that it is well away from the boat
*   throw rubbish into the sea

Finally, if you see anyone behaving irresponsibly around whales, report them to the proper authorities or to an appropriate conservation group.

A NOTE ON PHOTOGRAPHY

Most of the photographs in this book were taken on commercial whale watching trips during 1992/93. I went on several hundred altogether, varying in length from a couple of hours to nearly two weeks. The only exceptions were in South Africa, where I worked exclusively from land-based observation points, and in Sri Lanka, where the civil war made organised whale watching impossible.

I use Nikon equipment: one F4 and two F3s with motordrives and a range of lenses from 18mm to 1000mm. The most useful combination is undoubtedly the F4 with an 80-200mm autofocus lens. This is ideal for most species and conditions, although I often use both the camera and the lens on their manual settings. The few underwater pictures I took were on a Nikonos V with a 35mm Nikkor lens.

I use mainly Kodachrome 64 (rated at 80 ASA) and Kodachrome 200 slide film. The golden rule in whale photography is to try and forget the cost of the film and to keep taking pictures. There are always a great many rejects caused by boat movement and bad timing and, of course, on commercial trips a huge number of otherwise good shots are ruined by the hands, elbows and heads of fellow whale watchers. Motordrives are the best way of spending loads of money but, without them, you need a great deal of luck to capture the perfect moment with a single shot.

The best whale pictures are usually the ones that are not planned. Since whales tend to do the most sensational things when they are least expected (typically after a long lull in the action) it is a good idea to have a camera ready all the time. Otherwise, it is easy to be caught with the equipment packed away in a bag, in the middle of changing a film or queuing up for the bathroom when something out of the ordinary happens.

Whales, of course, live in the sea which, unfortunately, is wet and salty. Both water and salt can ruin camera equipment, so cameras and lenses must be properly protected from the elements. I use a tough Pelican case, which is 100 per cent waterproof, but even a strong plastic bag is better than nothing.

Finally, a simple request. Please remember that no picture is more important than the safety and welfare of the whales themselves.

FURTHER INFORMATION

If you would like to support efforts to protect the world's whales, write to:

The American Cetacean Society,
National Headquarters,
P.O. Box 2639,
San Pedro,
California 90731, USA.

The Whale & Dolphin
Conservation Society,
Alexander House,
James Street West,
Bath, Avon BA1 2BT, UK.

There are many excellent books available on whales, but the following should be of particular interest to anyone wishing to find out more about some of the places or species mentioned in *On the Trail of the Whale*:

Alan N. Baker, **Whales & Dolphins of New Zealand & Australia: An Identification Guide**, Victoria University Press, 1990.

Ben Bennett, **The Oceanic Society Field Guide to the Gray Whale**, Sasquatch Books, 1989.

Michael A. Bigg, Graeme M. Ellis, John K. B. Ford and Kenneth C. Balcomb, **Killer Whales**, Phantom Press, 1987.

Patricia Corrigan, **Where the Whales Are: Your Guide to Whale Watching Trips in North America**, The Globe Pequot Press, 1991.

Eric Hoyt, **The Whale Watcher's Handbook**, Penguin / Madison Press, 1984.

Eric Hoyt, **Orca: The Whale Called Killer**, Camden House 1990.

Gregory Dean Kaufman & Paul Henry Forestell, **Hawaii's Humpback Whales: A Complete Whale Watcher's Guide**, Island Heritage Publishing, 1986.

Margaret Klinowska, **Dolphins, Porpoises and Whales of the World: The IUCN Red Data Book**, IUCN, 1991.

Stephen Leatherwood, Randall R. Reeves and Larry Foster, **The Sierra Club Handbook of Whales and Dolphins**, Sierra Club Books, 1983.

Anthony R. Martin, **Whales and Dolphins**, Salamander Books, 1990.

Bruce Obee and Graeme Ellis, **Guardians of the Whales**, Whitecap Books, 1992.

Barbara Todd, **Whales and Dolphins of Kaikoura, New Zealand**, Craig Potton Publishing, 1991.

Mason T. Weinrich, **Observations: The Humpback Whales of Stellwagen Bank**, Whale Research Press, 1983.